High Kicks

The essential guide to working as a dancer

Donna Ross

A & C Black • London

044

First published in 1999
by A & C Black (Publishers) Limited
35 Bedford Row, London WC1R 4JH

ISBN 0-7136-5110-5

A CIP catalogue record for this book is available from the
British Library.

The Publisher has made every effort to contact the copyright
holders of the photographs used in this book. In some cases
this has not proved possible and the publisher apologises to any
copyright holder whose work has been used without specific
permission.

Cover photograph: Hilary Shedel / Arena Images
Page design by Judith Gordon

Typeset in 10.5 on 12pt Janson
Printed in the United Kingdom by
Biddles Ltd, Guildford and Kings Lynn.

Contents

Author's note

The dancing industry as it stands is predominately female, and throughout the book I refer to the dancer as 'she' and to the client, agent and choreographer as 'he'. As an agent myself I am aware that both sexes work in all these occupations; this style has been used purely to avoid cumbersome alternatives such as 'he/she'.

Acknowledgements

I have used my own experiences as the main source of information and research for this book, but none of it would have been possible without some of the people I've met along the way.

I owe a huge thank you to all my great dancing friends, some of whom have contributed to this book: Sue, Helen, Harri, Sam, Lotte, Alicia (Lula), Michelle, Lene, Lisa J, Lisa S, Aicha, Claire, Miranda, Alex, Lyndon and David. Thanks to all of you, especially those who worked silly hours through thick 'n' thin to get X-Directory, Dance Attic Productions and Essential off the ground. Also, to those who helped squeeze me into a catsuit again after giving birth! What fun we had being dancers!

Thank you to choreographers Priscilla and Kevan for the time and advice they have given to the future generations of dancers; to Steve Springford for his essential career advice, friendship and contacts; and to Andrew and Dee Dee for their help and studio space, but mainly for their trust and belief in my ventures! Thank you to Mum and Dad for supporting my dancing career every inch of the way (especially financially) and for helping me with all my decision-making! To my tremendously laid-back husband and best friend Trevor who is always my backbone and punchbag in whatever I do. Thank you darling! And to our children, Molly and Tommy, to whom I dedicate *High Kicks*, should they want to follow in Mummy's footsteps!

Foreword

by Dee Dee Wilde

What a marvellous idea! I should have thought of it, but didn't. So well done Donna, full marks for execution and completion. Of course, this is a must for any young dancer starting out in what is a most precarious and competitive career. If you have the knowledge and advice of a useful little book like this, then you're streets ahead of the others. You need to be and you need all the help you can get. When I was starting out as a young dancer I knew nothing. I learnt the hard way. A book like this would have got me to the top in no time, but history decreed it would take a little longer! Of course, dancing these days is much more accessible; there are many more classes and excellent teachers around and a wider scope of dance too. The snag is . . . the competition is huge. You have to be able to do everything, even swing from chandeliers! But if this isn't daunting, and you have true grit and determination, there is no reason why you shouldn't succeed. Armed with this kind of ammunition and Donna's book, how can you fail? What to do, who to see, where to go, it's all here along with a few helpful hints from us old pros. Once you've made it, I hope you enjoy being a professional dancer as much as I did, I had a ball! The best of British luck . . . AND KEEP ON DANCING!

Introduction

Being a dancer has got to be one of the most exciting jobs in the world – there is nothing else like it. The satisfaction gained from getting up in the morning to go and do what you love, spending a day in the studio with the music cranked up, pushing your body to the limit, expressing yourself and being paid for it is awesome! It is a far cry from rushing to a stuffy office or standing behind a counter, and I know, I've tried both.

I finally hung up my shoes to write this book, which I hope will enlighten dancers about the reality of the dance industry. *High Kicks* is designed to inspire you, but at the same time alert you to the pitfalls of the dancing profession. Whether it's fame you want or a steady career, it gives you, the potential dancer, a head start, revealing secrets and tips that I and other experienced dancers learnt the hard way.

I graduated from The London Studio Centre in 1989 as a professional dancer and ploughed through my career to accomplish my dancing ambitions. I've been on a film set in –2°C at 5.30a.m. wearing a corset and a hooped petticoat, ready to collapse from hypothermia; I've been in a warm, plush television studio, next door to Chris Evans' dressing room, wearing a little black number and ready to dance my two-minute routine on TFI Friday; I've been at the end of the queue at The New London Theatre waiting for the latest *Cats* audition; and, surprise surprise, I've been climbing the walls at home waiting for the phone to ring!

It wasn't until recently, when I was taking my four-year-old daughter Molly along to her much-loved ballet class, that it suddenly dawned on me what I must have put my parents through when I stamped my foot and announced I was going to London to become a dancer. Not only do I therefore sympathise with young dancers who have no contacts in the industry, but I understand the panic parents feel about their children's future income coming from a career that doesn't involve sitting at a desk or wearing a uniform!

How many times have you heard parents say, 'If you want to be a dancer, I think you should work hard at school and get your GCSEs and perhaps a degree, and if you still want to dance after that then you can'. Whereas if you said, 'I want to be a doctor' they would be more than delighted to back your decision and help you on your way to medical school. Sound familiar? As much as I protested to my dad against the need for an education when all I wanted to do was dance, in actual fact he was right. It's probably all you've ever wanted to do, but dancing as a hobby is very different to vocational dancing.

I founded Dance Attic Productions five years ago with Dee Dee Wilde. It is now The Essential Agency Ltd, one of London's leading dance agencies, and owned by Fred and Richard Fairbrass of the band 'Right Said Fred'. As an agent I am astounded how little dancers know about their chosen career. Every time I interview a dancer for representation I tell them something that they don't know about the industry, even those with years of training and employment.

This book is primarily a link between learning to dance and branching out into the professional field. It does not teach you how to dance, but how to work as a dancer. It also acts as a handbook, to be referred to throughout your career, and which professional dancers can use to refresh their memories or re-establish themselves after time away from the industry. Everything within the commercial field of dancing is covered: preparing to become a dancer; working as a dancer; and the business of being a dancer. I explain where you can train, how to prepare CVs and photographs, what you should wear to auditions and how to get an agent, and I have called on friends and established choreographers to share their experiences. I discuss all the types of commercial work available, not to mention the accounting side of the business!

Successful dancers can receive tremendous rewards, earn a good living and dance all over the world, and it is the ones who persist and have the will to get on who will be chosen. You need the talent and dedication to survive in a career full of knock-backs, and enough determination to let people judge you day in and day out, telling you you're too short, too fat, or your arms are too hyper extended! *High Kicks* shows you how to become a skillful 'working' dancer. Your dancing career will present so many decisions and emotions, most of which I have faced and will share with you. You have chosen a rollercoaster career, not a normal merry-go-round job, and you face a ride of incredible highs and lows on your journey to success. With the right attitude and dedication, however, this essential guide will show you the way to fulfil your ambitions and make it as a successful dancer. Enjoy the ride – it's a good one!

Part One
Preparing To Become A Dancer

Everybody wants to make a career out of something they love doing, and if you can achieve it, you will be content for the rest of your working life. Being a professional dancer is a fulfilling occupation, but by no means an easy one.

Preparing to become a professional dancer will take some time. Some of the dancers on television may look as if they have come straight from a club, but in actual fact they have trained for years to look that 'cool' and make dancing seem that easy. Commercial dancing in particular uses 'street' styles of choreography – steps you would be better off picking up at a club or literally 'off the street'. However, combining these steps with the perfected technique of classical ballet, jazz and contemporary dance at a professional level is a different matter. To reach the level of a musical theatre or television dancer takes concentrated preparation. Can you developpé your leg to 90°? Do you know what a 'Z card' is? Do you need an agent? Have you ever been to an audition? This section will give you the answers to these questions, plus a knowledge of how to go about training, develop your image, get a CV and photographs together, and get 'seen' at auditions – everything it takes to become ready to work as a dancer!

Chapter One

Training

The need to train

First things first. It is assumed that if you are reading this book, you have dreams of becoming a professional dancer. It is also assumed that you have had some dance training already, either from attending your local dancing club or going to classes. Having a general background knowledge of dance and a passion for it is a great start. All you need to do now is shed blood, sweat and tears, in other words train!

You *do* need to train, although some people think otherwise with the recent increase in the popularity of 'street dance' within the industry. Without a strong dancing technique you will be limited in the type of work you can do, whereas fully trained dancers can go from strength to strength.

It is wise to train full-time for at least a year if you are considering a dancing career and it is not advisable to audition before you are ready. Training is a complete programme designed to build up your stamina and develop your muscles to resist against injury and prepare your body and mind for dancing at the highest level. There are a number of ways you can train for your career, and it is necessary to do some research into the different types of training courses available to see which is best suited to you as an individual. For example, a dancer who has trained classically from the age of three may not need such intense training as someone who took up jazz as a teenage hobby. Only you can decide which type of dance training will be suitable, and find the college or class to train at, and this will depend on:

- the standard of dancing you've reached
- where you live
- who is paying the fees
- which course you are accepted on.

Once you have done some research and investigated what is on offer at each college or studio, it will become apparent which one(s) you should apply to.

Going to college

A potential dancer needs to work her body every day, and college is the perfect venue for this. Most dance colleges cover the major disciplines of classical ballet, musical theatre and contemporary dance, and if you are considering commercial work you must train extensively in at least one of these categories. Generally, dancers who leave school at 16 having danced part-time for a few years, choose to do a three-year course at an accredited college. Advanced dancers, for example those who have previously attended stage school, may decide to take a one-year graduate course, or perhaps avoid going to college and train freelance, taking classes at a professional studio every day.

Applying for college

The first thing to do is obtain a prospectus from a selection of colleges. Telephone or write, expressing your interest, and then find time to mull over each one before you make any decisions. The prospectus will reveal information which will help you narrow down your choice. It will give a history of the college, a list of successful students who have attended, examples of timetables, photographs of their facilities, and most importantly the fees per term. Before you go any further imagine yourself at one of the colleges, picture yourself going there every day for the next three years.

- Do you like the location?
- Do you like the range of classes available?
- Do you get a good first impression from reading about the place?

Don't be too quick to accept the first college. Although it is tough to get into college, they all need business and recruit many new students every year. You have as much chance as the next dancer. Whatever you decide make sure it is right for you. Don't be persuaded to go to a particular college just because you heard about it on television. Talk to dancers who have begun their training and find out the success rate of the college(s) of your choice – what percentage of dancers who graduated are working professionally? You must make sure you know what is on offer at each college; you may want to cover Speech and Drama or Stage Management in case your career takes a diversion, so make sure they cover it.

The next step is to write to your chosen college(s) and ask for details on funded places and scholarships and an application form. You will be sent a reply outlining the procedure through which to obtain possible funding along with the application form, and you will need to complete the form and return it with a photograph of yourself and an audition fee which covers the administration and refreshments for the audition day.

Try and audition for more than one college to avoid disappointment. Unless you are adamant that there is only one place for you, I suggest applying to three colleges to be sure of a place. You will then be sent a date and details of what you should prepare for the audition and what to bring with you. This is your chance to make an impression so think hard about how to approach your audition day.

Funding college

Financial considerations may influence your choice. College fees are not cheap and taking a professional class each day can amount to almost as much. Before you accept a place on any course, find out what is available to cover the costs.

Contact your local authority to find out if they award grants to fund vocational dance training. College fees are high as they receive no government funding, and many local authorities are reluctant to cover the cost of these courses. Some only award discretionary grants to courses accredited by the Council for Dance Education and Training (CDET). A limited number of awards for funded places will be available and the CDET provides a list of the accredited colleges. They also constantly update information on funding as the Government announces it. Send a stamped addressed envelope for the latest information sheets (see 'Listings'). If a funded place is available at the time you apply, you may need to do a separate audition for the authorities; places will be awarded to the most talented students. If you fail to qualify, you may be able to appeal or reapply the following year. Some colleges also offer scholarships which will cover your fees alone.

In addition to the tuition fees, however, you must account for living expenses. Don't forget to consider the travelling distance to the college you choose. Do you need to move into digs? Do you need to travel by public transport each day? If so, will you have the time and energy to work part-time to pay for these extra expenses? Be realistic otherwise life will be miserable, talk through the finances with your parent or guardian to help plan your time as a student.

Auditioning for college

College auditions can be pretty grilling, often lasting all day. They begin with a classical barre and general warm-up to relax everyone before nerves completely get the better of you. Auditions vary but can include the following.

(1) A medical – a nurse will test your general health and feel your joints, hips and spine
(2) A warm-up – usually a ballet barre
(3) Learning a jazz routine – to be performed in small groups to the judges
(4) A dance improvisation section – to demonstrate your musical interpretation
A break for lunch
(5) Singing a song of your choice
(6) Acting a classical and modern speech of your choice – performed not read
(7) An interview with the principals to find out about your personality

It is an ordeal, but be comforted by the fact that they are not expecting you to be perfect – if you were you wouldn't need to train! You must show potential and have a positive attitude.

The criteria for their assessment of you is usually several, if not all, of the following:

• musicality
• physique
• concentration
• responsiveness
• sense of dance and quality of movement
• expressiveness.

If these qualities shine through you will be accepted. If you didn't do too well on the improvisation, try and forget it and concentrate on the song you're doing next. The audition will normally include a brief interview with the principals at the end of the day. They will ask you blunt questions which may make you want to run out crying, like 'If you are unsuccessful, what will you do?' or 'Why do you think you should be accepted on this course?' Hold it together; they are testing you as you need a strong character to succeed! So what if they tell you your singing was off-key or that you need to lose a stone? As long as you showed potential it doesn't matter. Like any test you can have 'off' days which may result in failure, but don't let it deter you. Stick at it – you can do it. Stay positive and every time they ask you a question answer with a happy, positive response. Try not to hesitate or answer with 'I don't know'. They won't feel sorry for you; the competition is too great for them to be sympathetic.

At the end of the interview some colleges will tell you if you have been successful, while others send you home to await a reply in the post.

What to expect at college

College can be a long endurance test and you will be pushed to the limit. Most good training programmes will include a two-hour ballet class first thing in the morning. It doesn't matter if you are on the musical theatre course, classical dance provides an excellent grounding for you to build the rest of your art around. It gives you a recognised technique, excellent posture and discipline, and is the foundation necessary for a strong, toned, flexible dancer who wishes to succeed in the commercial field of dancing.

Classes will start around 8.30a.m. and go on until 6p.m., with further rehearsals for productions outside college hours and at weekends. The following timetable shows the wide range of subjects available.

MONDAY	TUESDAY	WEDNESDAY	THURSDAY	FRIDAY
Ballet	Ballet	Ballet	Ballet	Ballet
Street Jazz	American Tap	Matt Mattox	Rock Jazz	Contemporary
Pointe Work	Pas De Deux	Singing Harmonies	Improvisation	Shakespeare Drama
Voice	Spanish	Character	Body Control	Diet and Nutrition
Television	Acting	Musical Theatre	Voice	Classical Repertoire
Anatomy	Grand Allegro	Musical Staging	Mime	Make-Up
National	Luigi Jazz	Adage	Mask Work	Choreographic Workshop

The broad spectrum of subjects gives a full range of dance styles and theatre techniques, covered in enough detail over two or three years of training to prepare students for the outside world. There is so much to cover and learn and every student normally organises her own timetable to include certain subjects. It is better to have a sound base in one or two dance forms that you do every day (e.g. ballet and jazz) and then add other subjects to your timetable which will help you become a flexible performer (e.g. singing, tap and drama). Some lessons are theory, but 80 per cent of the training is physical and you will have to go from class to class giving 100 per cent effort to each teacher. At the end of the training programme you should feel ready and hungry to work, and be in great shape with the stamina to run a marathon!

PHOTO: HILARY SHEDEL/ARENA IMAGES

Classes

Most dance lessons begin with a head-to-toe warm-up before any dancing starts. In ballet this will be barre work, while some teachers may ask you to do your own brief warm-up if they know you have had lessons earlier. In each class the warm-up is followed by a series of exercises and sequences to learn new dance steps. They are often strung together and danced across the floor, or performed in groups to add variety to the class. Finally a routine is taught and sections of choreography are pieced together to create a dance.

Classes have the same basic format, similar to those you will have been doing up to now; the difference is that they accelerate to a professional level and the teachers expect nothing less than 110 per cent effort. At this level there is no room for timewasters. Professional teachers don't wish to know how tired you are, or the problems you are having in your personal life. Forget your troubles when you turn up to class, get focused and indulge in the music and rhythms. You will discover muscles you never thought you had and 'step ball change' suddenly becomes 'grand jeté en tournant'! This intense training will change you from an amateur into a fully conditioned professional.

The satisfying feeling you get from working hard in class gives a fabulous sense of achievement; your teacher pushed you to produce results and pulled a performance from you that you never thought possible. You can feel that way every day if you put in the hours, and that's when the results will pay off!

Professional dance studios

If you have had a good background training in dance as a child and cannot get into a college for whatever reason, regular professional-level classes at a dance studio may be the answer for you. They usually have a large number of fully equipped dance studios with sprung floors, mirrors and barres, purpose-built for training, auditioning and rehearsing. Freelance classes at these studios include regular jazz, ballet and tap classes, ranging from beginners to advanced, while a wide range of other classes may also be on offer, from flamenco, body-popping and locking, and pointe work, to Tai Chi, Yoga, and Kung Fu. The most economical way to train is to buy membership to one studio and do one or two classes every day.

This is also a great way of making contacts in the industry as you get to meet choreographers and other dancers. Studios are also hired by record, theatre and television companies to rehearse their productions, and you may find yourself rubbing shoulders with pop acts rehearsing their concert tour or Andrew Lloyd Webber auditioning for his new creation. Studios usually include a fitness gym and a coffee bar, an excellent way to absorb the atmosphere and make and meet friends in-between the hard work.

Student training at the London Studio Centre

PHOTO: IAN TURNER

Points to remember

- Research all the types of training available before rushing into a decision.
- Read the prospectuses of a few colleges to compare them and find out more about them.
- Imagine yourself at the college you select – do you like the location and the timetable of classes?
- Find out about funded places and scholarships that may be available.
- Contact your local authority to see if they award grants for vocational training in your area.
- Audition for more than one college if possible.
- Consider travelling distance to the college or studio you choose.
- Remember to account for living costs while you're a student.
- Show off your best qualities and have a positive attitude when you audition for college.
- Remember they want raw talent, not perfection – they are looking at your potential.
- A strong dance technique will give you more options of work.
- Classical dance provides an excellent foundation for all dance styles, no matter how funky!
- Stick at your training however exhausted you are feeling – it *will* be worth it.
- Experience the wide range of classes at a professional studio and get a taste of the industry.

Chapter Two

Finding Work

How to find work

There are no set rules of how to obtain work and you have to be prepared to do some investigating. Finding work will be an ongoing procedure throughout your career. Few jobs last forever and even long dancing contracts can become tedious for a professional dancer. You may want to experiment in different areas of the industry and change from theatre to TV or dancing abroad. Begin by finding the publications that list job vacancies, talk to other dancers about forthcoming auditions and learn how to get your face seen, even advertise yourself in casting books.

You must also learn to distinguish between good work and bad. Be aware of certain types of advertisements for jobs. You will eventually develop your own means of avoiding pitfalls and finding out about legitimate auditions, but to find good work you need to think about promotion. This doesn't mean hiring a public relations company and launching a personal campaign, but compiling a set of details known as your promotional material or simply your CV and photo, which will entice clients into meeting you. Once you are in front of them you can then rely on your dancing talent to get you work. It is a common fact that to find work you need to be in the right place at the right time. You can't possibly be in a hundred places at once – but your CV and photograph can! Mailing out your promotional material will ensure you are invited to auditions and your face is noticed.

For most types of occupation you need academic exams to be considered for a job interview; for dancing work your dancing experience counts for everything. Thus the infamous 'chicken and egg' situation develops for dancers: you need a job to become experienced and you need experience to get a job. However, someone out there wants you to dance for them; you just need to know where to find them, how to convince them to audition you and how to make them choose you!

Get into the habit of looking and listening out for work. Keep promoting yourself and stay focused and positive in your search for success.

Promotional material

Promotional material is made up of your curriculum vitae (CV), your photograph and a covering letter to introduce yourself. It is essential to have these items with you throughout your professional career, and not just one set but several updated versions along the way. It is the key to getting private auditions, as clients usually like to consider who might be suitable for a job by reading dancers' details before inviting them along to audition. They like to mull over photographs and show them to their colleagues beforehand. This keeps numbers to a minimum and if a photo is readily available it helps the client cast the dancers. Your promotional material must be well presented. First impressions count and it is important to have decent photographs – a bad photo can be worse than none at all! A holiday snapshot and a hand-written CV are not good enough. You must invest in a good up-to-date professional photograph and a typed CV. The initial cost can be expensive, but it is worth getting it right. You may be able to pay for it with just one job, so it is a worthwhile investment.

Promotional material will eventually become like a passport – whether you bump into a friend who is on her way to see a choreographer or end up at an audition you knew nothing about until you turned up for class, it is essential you have your photo and CV handy to pass on to potential employers. One day your details will end up on the desk of someone who will open the door to your career, but without circulating them it will never happen. A dancer who works just by word of mouth and has no promotional material is either extremely talented or lucky. Having said that, I know a few dancers with excellent experience, whose reputations go before them and who no longer need promotional material – they are invited to auditions at the mere mention of their name. This is unlikely to happen early on in your career, however, so this chapter will advise you how to gather the relevant material and promote yourself in various ways to help you find work.

Photographs

Promotional photographs are your ticket to auditions and it is important to have an excellent professional shot which is a true reflection of you.

It doesn't have to show all your impurities, but it mustn't be so bleached out that you look like Kate Moss! If you look too good you may disappoint your client when he sees you in the flesh. Your photograph must be sharp (in focus), clear, interesting and versatile yet simple – not too fussy or detailed. It is a good idea to have a flattering body shot too, but take one step at a time; the photo you use initially should be your best one. Don't use a mediocre body shot just for the sake of it; wait until you get the right shot. Eventually you can work on building a portfolio and a composite or Z card (see page 29).

Before you run off to the nearest photographer's studio, try the following exercise: stand in front of a full-length mirror in a leotard and be honest with yourself by answering the following questions:

- Are you on the skinny side?
- Are you a bit chubby?
- Are your muscles toned?
- Are you short, average or tall?
- Is your face round, oval or square?
- Do you have high cheek bones or a square jaw?
- Are your legs long?
- Is your body long?
- Do you have a defined waistline?
- How does your hair look?
- Do you remind yourself of anyone (someone famous, or your mum perhaps)?

The answers to the above questions will determine your basic body structure – not the make-up, hair styles or clothes, but the you behind the cosmetics! Next write down your idea of a dancer's physique, again just the body shape. Finally, compare the two and see how many similarities there are. This is not designed to give you a complex about your body, it is purely to show you the parts of yourself that match the standards of your ideal dancer's shape. These are the parts that should be emphasised in your photographs as selling points. It's cruel, but true – you are the product and if it means you have to show off your great legs in your photographs to get work, then do it!

The photographer

You must choose the right photographer for your requirements and the phone numbers of several recommended photographers can be obtained from the listings section at the back of this book. It is important you use a photographer with a good reputation for shooting dancers' portfolios. A local portrait photographer who specialises in weddings will not take the right pictures. You need sharp, professional photographs to give you plenty of career opportunities.

The best way of finding a photographer is to talk to other dancers and get recommendations, then make a series of phone calls before you actually commit yourself to a session. Have a list of questions you want to ask written down in front of you before you make your phone calls. Don't forget to ask for the location of the photographer's studio – is it convenient for you to get to with your wardrobe and new hair style in the rain?

Occasionally you hear bad reports about photographers, and unfortunately there are some cowboys who have ulterior motives for taking your photograph. Be especially aware of photographers who advertise in newspapers with phrases like: Models required – no experience necessary! It is always a good idea to visit your chosen photographer prior to your session date to have a chat. Look at his work, tell him what you like and don't like, then bounce your ideas off him so he can tell you if they are possible. Remember, you are the paying customer so don't put up with things you don't feel comfortable with.

The cost

Prices vary between photographers and depend on what you want to have done. You will be charged a general sitting fee for the studio time alone, then the cost of the film and the photographer's fee which is usually based on their expertise and experience. In addition to this you may need a make-up artist, a stylist or a hairdresser, depending on what you are trying to achieve. As a very approximate guide you can spend £35–£55 for a basic session and £100–£300 for more. It is best to make a series of phone calls to get realistic quotes.

Photographers usually put together package deals for dancers and sometimes offer a promotion where they will add in free extra prints or film. Such a package might include: 2 x black & white rolls of film, 1 x colour roll, a make-up artist/stylist, a free 10 x 8 print and 10% discount if you order more than ten prints.

The photo session

Before you book your photo session talk to other dancers and look at their pictures and through magazines to inspire you and give you ideas for clothes and poses. It can be awkward posing for your first set of photographs and you may wish to make use of props to give you something to hold. Standing in front of a white backdrop trying to look natural is extremely difficult unless you are experienced in creating good poses. Take a friend along on the day of your photo session, especially if she is a dancer too, as she will tell you if your tummy is sticking out or your trousers are twisted. Although it is the photographer's job to think of these things, they are often too concerned about their lighting and shadows to notice your minor details. Use the following ideas to make your photographs more interesting.

- Make use of props and furniture – try sitting the wrong way round on a chair or leaning against its back.
- Lean against a brick wall.
- Visit a park and play around to get natural fun shots.
- Try an action shot – leaping in the air or kicking your leg.
- Sit on a box or step-ladder to give you a change of level and a greater choice of camera angles.
- Take along a CD or cassette of your favourite music and ask the photographer to play it to create atmosphere.
- Use clothes such as a baggy shirt to hold, take off, or drape over yourself.
- Use large hair clips – start off with your hair up then let it down during the shoot.
- Use a wind machine for a different effect.
- Find some poses that show your agility and flexibility.
- Change location or background for each different look.
- Play up to the camera – exaggerate facial expressions and have some fun to create energy.

Clothes

You have to make certain decisions about what to wear in your photographs. Beware of trends that may pass quickly and date your photos, leaving you embarrassed to use them 12 months later if the clothes you're wearing have gone way out of fashion. Take a large selection of clothes with you, especially if you haven't got a stylist, and practise at home beforehand to get a good idea of which outfits you want to wear.

Choose clothes that flatter your shape. For example, if your trunk is toned then wear a mid-rift top, while boys with great definition may want to go bare-chested for some photographs. The competition is tough for dancers and while you may look great in jeans and trainers at home, for work you must look great in tight-fitting costumes and in your promotional photographs. If you have a particularly athletic body then it is a good idea to plan some flattering body angles for your promotional shots. Take into account colours and textures – colours that clash may work wonders on black and white film. Talk it through with your photographer – he knows best.

PHOTO: SERGIO BONDIONI

Hair and make-up

Hair and make-up should also be given careful consideration and a good make-up artist will advise you on tones to suit colour or black and white film. If you do your own make-up, don't plaster it on, just emphasise your everyday make-up and use extra finishing powder to avoid shining under the lights. Your hair should be well groomed and worn however it suits you best. Never have your hair cut just before a shoot as fringes can look severe and boys' cuts can look harsh. Plan it so that you have at least a couple of weeks' growth. If your hair is long enough to put up try a few different styles but avoid suddenly turning into a supermodel and having your photographs looking nothing like you. It is easy to let your imagination run riot, especially if you have an extravagant make-up artist helping you. Unless you can portray the same look when you walk in the audition room, make sure that your promotional photographs reflect the real you. It is infuriating for casting directors if they see your photograph, yet when they see you in the flesh there is no comparison. The photo you use the most should be your fresh, clear and true-to-life reflection.

Portfolio and Z cards

A portfolio is a display book of a selection of your photographs – a professional version of a photo album. It is usually an A4 or A5 hardback display book containing a selection of black and white and colour shots that show your versatility with a range of different looks. This is when a mixture of wild hair dos and zany clothes can be put to use! A portfolio is a model's bible and is used by dancers who apply for photographic and body work. Your portfolio should be compiled over a period of time and updated whenever possible. Perhaps you worked on a hair show and had photographs taken; if you can get a copy from the photographer it would be great for your portfolio as it would show a different image of you and the job you did.

A Z card or composite (sometimes called an index card) is usually A5, double sided, and consists of one, or sometimes two, very clear shots on the front, with a selection of two to four shots on the reverse, portraying different images of you and your best qualities – legs, hair, cheeky face, character look, etc. There is a famous *French and Saunders* sketch about two 'luvvies' discussing their new 'cards'. They cut to a close-up of the card showing three identical clichéd shots but with three differences – with glasses, without glasses and with hands! Right idea, wrong photos.

Not all dancers find it necessary to use cards. Some use a single photograph, others use different photos for each job they apply for, depending which is most suitable. A popular shot is a one-sided double shot, i.e. one head and shoulders shot and one full-length shot side by side. Remember to label all photographs with your name printed clearly in bold letters on the front or hand-written on the back. It is a good idea to use name and address labels on the back of your photos. These are cheap to buy, compact and easy to read.

Reproductions

You will undoubtedly need copies of the photographs you give out and to order several copies of an original print will be costly. A reproduction photograph (or repro) is taken from an original print or negative and reproduced several times on photographic paper to look very much like the original, with only a small amount of quality lost compared to the original. Printing firms specialise in running off dozens of copies at a time as it is a cheaper process and you get more for your money. How many copies you order will vary; only you know how often you will change your image. The photos you send out must be a true reflection of you now, not five years ago. It can become expensive if you order hundreds of cards then get your head shaved! Apply a little thought to your photographs, for example if you regularly dye your hair only use black and white prints; if you constantly change your hair style have a card showing all the different styles;

PHOTO: SERGIO BONDIONI

or use a photograph which emphasises your face, perhaps with your hair gelled back. How many copies you order will also depend on how many you can afford. Greater quantities are better value for money, but only if you are going to use them. It is ridiculous to order less than ten if you are applying for work, but it takes a good while to work your way through 500! Remember, you *will* change even if it is only a result of growing older. Publicity photographs should be updated every 18 months if possible.

Curriculum vitae

A curriculum vitae (CV) is an account of your personal details – address, telephone number, height, hair and eye colour, and previous training and experience. It should be clear to read, not too long, and should reflect the type of dancer you are by showing where you trained and the work you have done. Limit your CV to one interesting A4 page rather than several pages of waffle. When you start out as a professional dancer you may have trouble trying to make your details fill the page, but when you do have more experience choose the most prestigious jobs to appear on it. It is far better just to list five impressive recent jobs than every Panto dating back to 1975! Personal details should be listed with spaces between each entry, while columns of text are the best way to detail your experience, for example the production you danced in (column 1), where it was made (column 2) and who you worked for (column 3), as shown in CV 1. If you don't have all the details of the job, for instance you don't know the name of the company you worked for, then it may be best to group similar work types together in categories, as shown in CV 2.

The correct way to write a CV has never been cast in stone. It really depends on the details you have and what you want to say. The secret is to present it well. Don't put your date of birth, age or playing range; leave it to the reader's imagination. If he knows your age it may affect his final decision. It is best to leave out dates altogether, as the reader may work out how old you are or wonder why you haven't worked for two years. Your best job may have been six years ago but it still looks great on your CV; including the date beside it may quash its credibility. Don't list hundreds of academic exams or all the ballet grades you've passed. The college or studio you trained at will tell the reader enough. Advanced dancing exams, scholarships and awards are sometimes worth mentioning, however. Use your common sense and only list relevant details. A choreographer doesn't need to know about your A Level in Home Economics!

Your CV must be updated more often than your photographs. It is a good idea to gain access to a word processor as it should always be typed rather than hand-written. A good quality paper should also be considered, maybe in a tasteful colour to catch the eye. Once again it is worth speculating on your initial promotional material – this is the launch of your career and presentation

Rosie Cheeks

Address:	72, The High Road	London W6 8AN
Telephone:	0181 000 6677	**Mobile:** 0987 654321
Height: 5' 6"	**Hair:** Blonde	**Eyes:** Blue
Training:	London Studio Centre	Performing Arts Scholarship

Theatre

Hans Anderson	Tunbridge Wells	David Smith
Dick Whittington	The Grand Wolves	Neil Thomson
Jim Davidson Show	Bristol Hippodrome	James Watson

Tours

High Life Show	Bosnia	SSVC
C.S.E. Show	Falkland Islands	SSVC
C.S.E. Show	Belize	SSVC

Television

AC/DC	Elstree	Triangle Video
Apex fares	Shepperton	Stark Films Ltd
S. Express	Pear Tree studios	Rhythm King
Parallel 9	Shepperton	BBC
People Today	BBC Manchester	BBC
Top Of The Pops	Elstree	Positiva
The American Match	Wembley	Channel 4
Harry Enfield	Fountain TV	Tiger Aspect
The Detectives	Camden Palace	Celador Prods.
First Sex	Canary Wharf	Channel 4
Emma	Luton Hoo	Meridian
Firelight	Bucks	Carnival Films
Ricky Martin	CD.UK	LWT
TFI Friday	Riverside studios	Ginger TV

Photographic

Rotary watches
British Gas
Daily Mirror
Bella magazine
Debenhams
L'Oréal hair products
Wella hair products

Skills

Swimming, Pointe work, Football, Computer literate, Scuba diving.

Dan Sing

Address:	101 Well Close			
	Liverpool			
	L10 2BS	Height:	6' 2"	
		Chest:	42"	
Tel:	0678 123 456	Waist:	32"	
Mobile:	0789 011123	Hair:	Brown	
Equity No:	F00115678	Eyes:	Brown	

Training Doreen Bird College of Performing Arts

Experience

Film & Television
Talking Telephone Numbers for Celador Productions
Stars In Their Eyes
Top Of The Pops for Aqua
Top Of The Pops for Billie
Halifax 'Happy Landings' Commercial
Hellmans Commercial
Firelight for Disney
Apollo 440 video
Billie video 'Because I Want To'

Theatre
Principal Boy in Snow White – The Bristol Hippodrome
Princes Trust 'Meat Loaf' Concert – Royal Albert Hall
VE Day in Hyde Park – London, choreographed by Dougie Squires
The Royal Variety Performance – London
Radio One Roadshow – Torquay
Beauty and the Beast – Dubai

Trade Shows
Trevor Sorbie Hair Show, Rembrandt Hotel – London
Adidas Spring/Summer range – Manchester
Nike Athletics – Japan
Fulda Roadshow – Hanover, Frankfurt
Cobella World Congress – London

Choreographers Worked With
Kim Gavin, Dougie Squires, Brian Rogers, George May,
Les Charles, Kevan Allen

Special Skills
Gymnastics, Acrobatics, Roller Skating/Blading, Fencing,
Stage Fighting

Example: CV2

is essential. When you are satisfied with the results, run off plenty of copies – you are going to need them!

Useful hints:

- Use one sheet of A4 paper only.
- Make sure your name stands out.
- Remember to include your contact address and telephone numbers at the top.
- Don't give false information (one day you will be caught out).
- Don't give dates.
- Use columns or grouped categories for clarity and easy reference.
- Present a printed CV.
- Update the information regularly.

Contacting employers

You have made a start by preparing your CV and photographs. The next step is to get your promotional material into the hands of future employers. It is essential to mail your details to various contacts and apply for work by post. If you are currently working in a theatre show for six months and you intend working when your contract ends, then keep in touch with people by writing one letter a week from your dressing room. Get into the habit of mailing out your details; it is the best way to follow up contacts as you start to meet people that could help your career.

Covering letter

A letter explaining who you are and why you are writing is as important as the promotional material you are enclosing. If you have gone to great lengths to have good photographs taken and a CV printed, it is pointless ruining your efforts by throwing them together in the post with a hurried, scribbled note. The presentation of your correspondence is an important factor and can reflect your personality. A tatty letter may suggest you are lazy or untidy, while details sent without a covering letter at all may seem stand-offish or unsociable. A good covering letter gives you a chance to introduce yourself and express your suitability for the job. Try to imagine being on the receiving end of your letter – would you be impressed? Although it is not always necessary to enclose a letter, it is polite to include a 'with compliments' slip at the very least.

Your letter should be short, sharp and legible. Try to include as much information in as few words as possible. Don't get carried away or write as if you are talking; this is a common mistake and a sure way of making your letter too long. Start by sticking to the basic letter writing rules:

- include your contact address and telephone number at the top of the page
- give the date
- begin the letter Dear Sir/Madam, or use their full title if known
- neatly lay the letter out within a margin
- use paragraphs
- end with 'Yours sincerely/faithfully' depending on who the letter is to.

Aim for a strong opening, an informative middle and a positive conclusion. You may have to make a few drafts of your letter before it is ready to send. Remember your letter is one among a large pile of others which also have to be read, so it is worth taking the time to get it right – it may get you the job.

Letters don't have to be typed; it sometimes adds a personal touch if your letter is neatly hand-written, contrasting with the printed details of your CV. If hand-writing is not your forte, however, stick to the word processor. Whichever method you choose, think about the paper you are writing on. It doesn't have to be the best quality Conqueror, but it should be flat and clean on departure. Tea-stained and dog-eared paper is not greatly appreciated. It is worth a visit to a stationer's and investing in a ream of writing paper, envelopes, paper clips, etc. Hard-back envelopes are most suitable, while clear folders are a great way of presenting your details in a neat, easy-to-read package. Your aim is to try and get your details seen amongst the competition and you must find a way of making your package eye-catching and appealing to the reader. Don't use yellow paper with black polka dots on it, however, and similarly wit should be used with caution – the casting director may not share the same sense of humour. Remember to enclose a stamped addressed envelope if you would like your details returned.

Once you are happy with your letter, make a copy to keep in your file and attach the original on top of your photograph and CV to avoid separation on arrival (make sure your name is on each individual item in case this does happen). Just before you send your details make a note in your diary of who you wrote to on which date and what you are applying for. Then if you receive an unexpected phone call days later you can refer back quickly and show your assertiveness.

Phone calls

It is sometimes appropriate to follow up your mail-out with a phone call 10–14 days later if you haven't already had a reply. Keep a record of who you have written to and file any replies for future reference. You may wish to reapply to a particular source in a year's time and want to compare that reply to the initial response. It is sometimes necessary to make a phone call to your contact before writing, however this should be avoided if possible. Busy clients don't know you personally and if they spent all day on the phone to you and a thousand others answering questions they would never get anything done. They much prefer you to send your details for them to look over when they have allocated time to do so. Pestering them on the phone will just reduce your chances of work. If you have a genuine question, be polite, brief and direct.

Casting books

A casting book is a directory of artistes, usually produced by agencies to show photos of the people they represent. The books come in all sizes and colours to make them as eye-catching as possible, and are generally updated annually, then circulated to thousands of clients. It is a form of advertising for both agent and artiste and casting directors frequently use them for casting commercials and so forth.

Dancers' details are also included in casting books, especially when good physiques are required for advertising. Next time you watch a commercial break on television or look at advertisements in a magazine, see how many images of a toned body are used. These are very often dancers' bodies.

You will have to pay for your own entry into a casting book as it is to promote you. The cost of appearing in a casting book usually depends on the agency compiling it and the total number of entrants. Sometimes you can pay for a quarter of a page or half page and so on and the price reflects on that. On average you won't see much change from £100 to appear in a book for approximately 18 months (remember to include it in your tax deductible expenses). Some agencies arrange for this fee to be deducted from work done through the agency.

Appearing in a casting book has the advantage of your photograph reaching clients and casting directors you don't know about and relieves you of constant mail outs. It is worthwhile for a client to flick through a casting book rather than attend to individual CVs and photographs piling up on his desk. It becomes a directory for the office and may be used several times a day.

It is a good idea to experiment with casting books, for example enter one book and see how much work you obtain from it in a year. Some agencies insist you enter their book to be with the agency. This is slightly unfair, but it does save a tremendous amount of administration if an agent can show his artistes in one complete file. It is important to choose a good clear photograph for a casting book as it will be circulated for at least 12 months.

Websites

With the increase of e-mail and the Internet, websites have recently become another method of 'getting seen'. Agencies are setting up casting pages and going 'on-line' for easier access to work abroad. Photographs and even moving images (such as excerpts from showreels) can be called up on the web by casting directors worldwide. While people are still slightly vague about the latest developments in technology and continue to use casting directories, dancers' photographs on the Internet are definitely a thing of the future. Some agencies use both methods for advertising and give free introductory offers to enable your photo to appear in a casting book and on a website. It's quite a buzz to go on-line and see your image on a computer screen.

Showreels

A showreel is a VHS video tape showing short excerpts from your previous experience. As a general rule, dancers don't really need a showreel; auditions are usually held to choose dancers as it is not easy to distinguish their standard on film. Dancers who use showreels as promotion are normally those with a fair amount of experience of professional TV and video work. They send their reels to potential employers instead of auditioning, especially if they are unavailable on audition day. Showreels are also beneficial for dancers who also sing and act, sometimes enhancing their chances of getting an agent. Showreels can be as short as one minute or as long as five minutes, but any more than this becomes tedious to watch no matter how good it is, and clients often have hundreds of videos to watch. A good showreel will show a dancer's versatility and present a compilation of different styles compactly edited together. It should portray energy and colour and the filming should be good quality – an out-of-focus home camcorder will not usually suffice. Never send a showreel out uninvited. Always write a letter first and mention that you have one should they like to see it.

Being in the right place at the right time

It is true that a part of your career will come down to a certain amount of luck, and that means being in the right place at the right time. Whether it is someone you bump into or an unexpected audition, it may be the best career move of your life. An important part of a dancer's job is to be 'out and about' making friends and contacts. Avoid becoming a hanger-on or a pest, but visit your agent and dance studio on a regular basis. You have heard the clichés: 'you need to get your foot in the door' and 'keep your ear to the ground', but they are true and you must start your professional career by listening to gossip and absorbing information about what is happening and where. If you don't yet have an agent then you may have to rely on word of mouth for a lot of your work – some of the smaller production companies use friends of friends for the majority of their filming work, especially for pop videos. They even go as far as picking hip-looking kids off the street. Be alert and make friends at auditions as an incredible amount of work is obtained by doing this. Dancers talk and often recommend each other as they build their own contacts; it is much more fun to work with a group of your friends. Apart from anything else, if you are relaxed in the company of friends the standard of dancing is much stronger.

Choreographers know hundreds of dancers, so as you get to know about individual choreographers, you must introduce yourself briefly and politely, as this will at least make you more familiar with them at the next audition you do for them. If you are based in a city you will soon realise that the network of dancers is relatively small and everyone knows each other.

The business of dance

Like any business there are basic rules you need to apply to get your dancing career up and running. Without these you will have to use a tiresome process of trial and error, but if you apply a little thought before taking action you will eventually save time and money. It is strange to think of yourself as a business when there is only you. You are the boss, the staff, the financier and the product all in one person, but you don't need to get bogged down with complicated business strategies, you just need to remember the basic rules. You will not be employed if people don't know about you and what you have to offer, so you must advertise yourself – get out there and be seen!

Speculation – you have to speculate to accumulate. Invest money into your business, however small the amount.
Information – research and gather knowledge from every source.
Dedication – dedicate time to your dreams; be conscientious.
Preparation and organisation – prepare a basic plan and make foundations you can build on.
Execution – execute every area of your career with a positive attitude and energy!

Points to remember

- Get a publicity package together.
- Avoid waffling in your cover letter. Get straight to the point.
- Make sure your CV is typed on good quality paper.
- Enclose a stamped addressed envelope for a reply.
- Make sure your photographs are an accurate reflection of you.
- Send reproduction copies rather than original prints.
- Mail out your publicity to agencies and job applications.
- After your initial mail-out, continue to write to potential employers.
- Read the situations vacant page in *The Stage & Television* weekly newspaper.
- Enter yourself into casting directories.
- Read the notice boards at rehearsal rooms and dance studios.
- Spend time in the cafes at these places, watch auditions and make friends.
- Take classes with teachers who choreograph and get to know choreographers.
- Check in with your agent if you have one.
- Make a phone call every day. Keep in touch with fellow dancers as news travels fast.

Chapter Three

Agents

What an agent does

An agent is not an employer, but seeks employment on your behalf. He is running a business and his job is to find you professional engagements of a high calibre and genuine nature. He must be at an equally high professional level as the dancers he represents, and act as an instigator, motivator and organiser. Having a good relationship with a conscientious agent will increase your chances of working. Many dancers manage their own careers without the need for an agent – for example, dancers who go into production shows abroad or work for one particular cruise ship company. Depending on the type of dancing work you want to do however, at some point in your career it will probably be necessary to join an agency. Clients prefer to book dancers through an agency, as they know the dancers will be professional, of a good standard, and it reduces their administration if they can rely on an agent to organise their dancers. The majority of commercial dancing jobs are found via agencies (advertisements, television shows, photographic), while some work primarily for the music industry (videos, concerts, promotional tours). Dancers who want to work as much as possible and cover every aspect of commercial dance should therefore consider finding an agent.

You must be aware of the type of agency before you sign up, and make sure they cover all aspects of dance work you want to be considered for. A dance agency is not the same as personal management; this is when you sign an exclusive contract to one agent/manager who pays individual attention to your career, and every job you do is discussed and negotiated via him and only him. Personal managers are not always suitable for commercial dancers. They are usually geared towards competent all-round performers who sing, act and dance and it is best to wait until you have a few years' experience before you try to obtain personal management. The advantage of not using a personal manager is that you can belong to as many agencies as you want. It is quite normal for dancers to belong to a few agencies to increase their chances of working. You may be one of 500 dancers on an agency's books, but don't be disheartened by this. An agency will be a small business run by few staff. They make money by taking commission from the fees you receive from the work they find you. That commission has to cover all the overheads and upkeep of an office and its staff. Sometimes this results in large numbers of dancers being represented as this ensures that there are enough dancers to meet demand and gives them a wide range of styles and looks on file to fit the brief (job descriptions).

The fact that you work through a pool of agents will allow flexibility in the work you do and the career decisions you make. You may decide to suddenly take off on a 6 month contract abroad!

Belonging to a large agency doesn't mean you get treated any differently – you can still build a relationship with your agent(s). It is essential you get to know them and pop into the office from time to time to say hello, or hand them your new photographs instead of mailing them. You have to remind them of your talents and looks. Invite them along to any productions you're in, even if they didn't get you that particular job. All this will be to your advantage as it will make them recommend you for other work.

Whether or not you *need* an agent is your decision. It is important to remember that agents are there to enhance your chances of work. This doesn't mean you place your career in their hands and wait for them to get you work. They cannot guarantee employment. If you use an agent you must work with them and continue to find your own contacts, calling on your agent for assistance when it comes to negotiating contracts or organising rehearsals for example. There are many other advantages to having an agent. The experience from the auditions they send you to will in itself be valuable. Private auditions organised by agents will also give you far more chance of landing the job; because of the smaller numbers of dancers auditioning you will receive more attention. Once you have managed to successfully work a few times for the agent you will find he will call you up for jobs without you having to audition. He will recommend you to clients, and can potentially open the doors to new areas and further your career.

How to get an agent

Getting an agent can be a catch-22 situation – you need an agent to get an audition, but you need an audition to get an agent! This is not always true, however, and eventually you will find a way of 'being seen' by an agency. It is a good idea to research some agencies before you apply to them. Agencies no longer need to be licensed which unfortunately means anyone could start up as an agent. You can check how long they have been trading by contacting the DTI (Department of Trade and Industry) if you are suspicious, but the best way is to talk to other dancers. Gossip will tell you all you need to know about an agency. It usually helps if you already know somebody with the agency and can find out the type of work they attract. Some agencies concentrate on musicals and theatre shows while others focus on pop videos and television work. The majority accept all kinds of dancing work and don't specialise. Inevitably dancers will say some agencies are better than others, but that will depend on how much work they have given them.

You have to persist to get accepted by a good agency. Most of them are bursting at the seams with applicants and you have to find a way of getting your CV and photo to the top of the pile. Unlike model agencies, you can't just walk into the office, show your portfolio, and if you 'fit the bill' sign up to the agency that day. To get into an agency you must either look out for advertisements for open agency auditions or apply in writing with your promotional material and a stamped addressed envelope for a reply. Not all agencies hold auditions for their books, and if they do they are annually or two yearly. Initially I would suggest trying a mail-out to five agencies you've researched, even if you plan to attend a forthcoming agency audition as well.

Once your details reach the agent there are several factors to take into account before you are even considered:

Are they recruiting new dancers at that time? You may have chosen a time when the books are closed. This means the agency refuses to look at any new dancers for a certain period (usually 6–12 months). This is unfortunate, but if they spent all their time looking at new dancers they would never find any work for the existing ones. Your details will probably be filed away or returned and your reply will state when the books reopen and you will be reconsidered.

Do you live within a 50-mile radius of the agency? This doesn't always matter as dancing contracts are worldwide, but some agencies prefer you to be accessible for last-minute auditions. For example, if you live in Newcastle and have been called for an audition in London with just three hours' notice you probably won't make it in time, and if you do make it and you're recalled the following day, you will need overnight accommodation. You may be able to work around this by using a friend or relation's address when applying and giving your mobile phone number – dancers will go where the work is.

Do you look right for the agency? You may be the most qualified, most fantastic dancer, but the quality of your promotional material will either make an agent read more or put them off completely. If you are starting out and cannot afford new professional photographs explain this in the letter, and if you firmly believe you will be a good investment for the agency ask for an audition before you are judged. Some agencies are reluctant to take on too many dancers with the same look. It can be an advantage to look similar to other dancers, especially for backing dancing jobs, but if an agent is swamped with short-haired blondes then he may only be recruiting a particular look he's short of.

Are you available to audition? Once your details have been looked at, the agency may want to see you dance before deciding if you are right for their books. They will send you a date and time by return of post and if you are not available you may miss the chance of joining the agency. Always telephone or write to explain your situation and they may be able to reschedule it.

All the above factors have absolutely nothing to do with your talent as a dancer, but rely on your looks, where you live and the time of year you apply to the agency. If you are lucky enough to get past this then the next stage is to prove your capability and suitability to the agent. If you have sent a clear, well-presented CV and photograph and you are fully trained with some experience, this may be enough to get you an interview straight away. If you have an excellent CV with a poor photograph this may also be enough to get you into the office. Once you have got an interview you still have to show them your dance style and ability. The agency may place you on the books anyway and insist you dance for them at their annual agency audition or they may try you out on a few auditions and turn up to watch you. If you have a very commercial or versatile look you may be invited to join the agency just for certain types of work. If this is the case, you can prove yourself as a dancer, rather than just as 'a look' once you have signed up and worked for them.

The interview

If you are called in for an interview, the agent already has some background information about you – they have watched you in a performance, or a casting director has recommended you, or your CV and photograph landed on his desk at the right time and you have been asked along for an informal chat.

Interviews are the perfect opportunity for you to express your personality. You don't have to read a script or dance or sing, you just have to chat. However, nerves can still dictate your behaviour and may cause you to waffle or worse still, dry up. The secret is to be as prepared as possible and stay relaxed before you enter the room. Keep your conversation positive. Don't um and ahh or answer with: 'I don't really know' or 'I don't mind'. Be decisive and don't interrupt or slouch in the chair. It is good to show you have a sense of humour, but don't come across as a sarcastic know-all. Lying is pointless as clients can check up on details later. Exaggerating a little may be the path to take. Think about the questions you are asked and take your time with your answers. You are trying to impress and make your interviewer relaxed in your company – they are only human after all!

If you do not hit it off with the interviewer or are not suitable for the agency you may be told to your face. Some agents don't have time for apologetic refusals or letters sent in the post and will save themselves the paperwork by being brutally honest in your meeting with them. If you're overweight but otherwise suitable for their books they may send you away for three months to lose weight; or they may pack you off to singing lessons for a year before they finally agree to represent you. It is hard to face facts and it can be upsetting, but they will be doing you a favour by strengthening your character and making you more determined.

Agents have a variety of personalities. You tend to imagine a rather overweight man in a leather armchair smoking a cigar whose first words are: 'So you wanna be a star?' This couldn't be further from the truth. Nowadays agencies are run by young, trendy, career-minded people who are terribly efficient and outgoing and work very long hours. They know how to talk to theatre companies and how to handle fussy production companies. More importantly they understand that you as a dancer want to, and need to, work hard and earn well. So when it comes to interviews they will be honest and forthright in telling you what they think. If you pass your interview with flying colours you may be asked to fill out details on the spot or you may be given documents to take home with you, read, sign and then return to the agency.

How agencies operate

Agents have different systems of operation, but the basic procedure is the same. All artistes will normally be kept on a computer database with their details set out for easy access. In addition to this the artiste will have a file for all her CVs and photographs or Z cards (they will request a certain amount of promotional material at your interview or when you sign up).

The agent will get a call for a job and a brief to go with it. He will then select the artistes he thinks will be most suitable for the job and telephone them all to make sure they are available. Some agencies have a 'booking out' system – if the dancer hasn't booked out he will assume she's available and automatically put her forward for work. It is nice to receive a call from your agent to let you know you are being recommended to clients, but it is too time-consuming for the agent as there may be 30 dancers to ring. The brief given may be for a dancer with a particular physique or a strong technique in an unusual dance style. It will basically be the client's vision described as well as possible to the agent. The agent will make suggestions to the client who will decide whether he wants to audition the dancers, look at their CVs and photos, or listen to the agent's spiel and book the dancers he recommends on the spot. If the client requests the dancers' details they may be faxed, posted, biked by courier or sent via the Internet (which is gradually becoming the best option). It all depends on the time-scale for organising the job. On receiving the details the client will select the dancers he would like to meet by means of a casting, interview or audition. If the client has called a number of agencies, the easiest way forward is to call an audition and invite a few dancers from each agency to ensure he gets the pick of the crop. The agent will then contact his dancers to give them details of the audition (time and place) and dates of the job should they be successful. You must try to be available on the end of a phone or have an answerphone at home to ensure you don't miss out on auditions. It is most infuriating for an agent when he can't track you down. He will phone your mobile (if you have one) to make sure he speaks to you. Have a pen and paper at the ready when he calls and write down all the details he gives you.

If you are chosen at the audition you must telephone your agent to tell him you have been selected. The client should also contact him, but it is best to phone anyway. At castings you won't find out until after the event, and the casting director will only call your agent if you have been successful. It is at this point that your agent moves into the driving seat. You have been through the tough procedure to get the job – now it is up to him to negotiate the best deal for you because that's what you pay him commission to do. The agent will organise everything from contracts and fees to travel to and from the job. You will receive a preliminary call to tell you the deal, then final confirmation or a contract later on. You will be asked to phone the agency the day before the engagement for your call time.

On completion of the job your agent will receive all payments (unless otherwise arranged) on your behalf. He will send an invoice, chase up the invoice, collect the payment, bank the monies, then reissue the agreed amount to you less his commission and possibly National Insurance or VAT depending on your contract. There are often all kinds of horror stories attached to agencies. They hold on to your money for months to gain interest in their bank account; they rip you off; they use you to make extra money. There *are* cases of dodgy agencies who have very suspicious ways of paying their artistes, but most reputable agencies are inspected by the DTI to ensure their payment system is appropriate and the artistes are paid within ten days of the agency receiving their money. It is usually the clients who ignore the 28-day terms of the invoice and give the agencies extra pressures, making them spend time reinvoicing, sending reminders and chasing them up to pay. However it's the agency that gets the complaints from dancers who desperately need to pay their rent!

Other than entering a casting book or going on a website (both for your own benefit) there are no charges for joining an agency. There should be no registration or administration fees and if these are mentioned in your interview then think again.

How to register

Agency contracts

When you are accepted by an agency, you will be given some forms to read and complete. You will be asked to fill out a database mandate with all your details, to be fed into their computer system, and you will be given a list of terms and conditions laid out by the agency of what they expect from their dancers. This will be in the form of a contract between you and the agency and covers both parties should any problems arise. These appear far more daunting than they really are and don't need a lawyer's approval (personal management contracts on the other hand are more complex). The contract is non-exclusive, as the agents are aware you will belong to other agencies, but it will ask you **to respect the fact that you will receive calls for the same audition from more than one agent.** The rules are the same for all the dancers on the books and special amendments won't be made just for you. The terms are usually straightforward and will only help you and your agent.

If you get called up by two agencies inviting you to the same audition you should accept the first caller. This often proves difficult as one agent will insist he left messages for you while the other spoke to you on your mobile. To avoid getting into an awkward situation be open and honest with both agents. It is painless to say, 'Sorry, I'm already going to that one'. Briefly disappointing for one agent, but far less hassle than accepting the audition from both. This can cause embarrassment later at the audition when your name is read out twice. And even more problems if you get the job! Your agents will be unaware of the situation and will start negotiations, thoroughly confusing the client and humiliating all parties, possibly resulting in no job and no agent at all!

Commission

All agencies charge commission. The amount will be made clear in your contract and usually varies between 10–25 per cent; it shouldn't be more. Some agents charge different rates for different jobs, for example, 10 per cent for theatre work, 15 per cent for television and video and 18 per cent for film and commercials. You must remember to take into account the commission you will have to pay when you accept a job; VAT may also be added to their percentage, so always work out or ask for the amount you will receive after deductions to avoid disappointment when you open your pay cheque.

Terms and conditions

To follow is an example of the terms and conditions laid out by an agent.

EMPLOYMENT
The agency is NOT your employer. You are a self-employed artiste and you employ the agency to find you work. You are responsible for your own income tax and National Insurance. National Insurance contributions may be deducted automatically at source from some contracts by law and any enquiries should be made direct to the DSS. Details cannot be provided for unemployment benefit, however, specific information can be supplied direct to artistes by making an appointment at the office. The agency agrees on recruiting an artiste to actively search for suitable work for them but does not hold any guarantee.

INSURANCE
The agency is not responsible for accidents or injuries which occur during your employment and advises all artistes to take out personal insurance. You may be covered on some contracts and be able to claim compensation should you suffer an injury.

UNIONS
We strongly advise all members of the agency to belong to a recognised union, e.g. The British Actors' Equity Association or The Musicians' Union. Although the agency will always act on

your behalf should a problem arise on a job and endeavour to rectify the situation, union regulations cover many more aspects of your work and give you reassurance.

BOOKINGS

If you have been pencilled or provisionally booked for a job we will confirm the booking as soon as possible, but if you want to accept alternative work during this time tell the office immediately so we can inform the client you are no longer available. ALL FIRM BOOKINGS MUST BE HONOURED. It is important to contact the office straight after an audition if you have been selected or if a client has told you he would like to book you. Never negotiate with clients direct – always ask them to contact us. It is unprofessional to discuss details when you have been booked via the agency. Any missed calls or auditions without a verifying reason will jeopardise your place on our books. It reflects extremely badly on the agency and may affect future bookings from the client. Please notify the office at the earliest moment if you are ill or have a problem so we can make alternative arrangements if possible.

COMMISSION

a) Theatre 10%.
b) TV and videos, trade shows, photographic 15%.
c) Feature parts, film and commercials 20%.

PAYMENT

All fees are confirmed at the time of the artiste's booking.

You the artiste have authorised the agency to collect payment on your behalf and deduct the agreed commission plus VAT at the current rate. Unless otherwise stated the payment procedure is as follows:

The agency endeavour to pay their artistes as quickly as possible. Payments are made by cheque only and take approximately 4–6 weeks to reach you from the date of engagement. Payment is issued to the agency who invoice on the day of engagement. Clients have a 28-day settlement period (reminders are automatically sent when the settlement day has been exceeded and steps are taken to chase outstanding fees). On receiving payments the agency take five working days for cheques to clear and then accounts are completed.

Payment to artistes are sent in the post with a remittance advice slip. This should be retained and kept for your tax purposes. A charge will be made for replacement copies.

The agency does not guarantee the payment of your fees by the client and is not liable for the responsibility of companies' non-payment or becoming bankrupt.

CONDUCT

The agency depends on the reliability and professional conduct of its artistes to keep its reputation going. Any artiste found under the influence of drugs or alcohol during employment will automatically be terminated from the files.

CHECKING IN

The agency office hours are 10.00a.m.–6.00p.m. Please make sure that you keep in contact with us every once in a while. If you have been booked on a job and are awaiting details please call in the day before to confirm the final arrangements – don't wait for the office to call you, especially if it is approaching the end of the day. Cancellations cannot be accepted outside office hours or left on the answerphone. A mobile number is available for **Emergencies only!**

APPOINTMENTS

When visiting the office PLEASE TELEPHONE FIRST. It is always nice to call in on us, but when ten dancers turn up at once it is impossible for us to stop and talk to everyone! Always make an appointment to ensure you get the necessary attention when coming in to see us. If you have any problems or questions regarding work, we are here to help you. We want to build a relationship between agent and artiste in order to further your career.

BOOKING OUT

If you accept a long contract, or are going to be unavailable for a long period, please let the office know the dates and 'book out' for the duration. If you change your appearance, e.g. cut or dye your hair, please let us know and provide new photos at your earliest convenience.

CONFLICTING ENGAGEMENTS

The agency appreciate you may belong to other agencies. If two agents phone you regarding the same audition, please make sure it is clear who is sending you.

REFERENCES

Typed references for artistes known to the agency for more than 12 months can be supplied at a cost of £3.50.

CASTING BOOK

The agency is currently compiling an updated casting book. It is important for all artistes to be included in this book, as it obviously increases your chances of getting work and not only provides clients with a professional photo of you, but saves you time and money in the long term, preventing unnecessary auditions or time-wasting journeys. Please sign the registration form and return it with a cheque for £95 and prints for the book.

THE AGENCY AUDITION

Annual auditions are held for the books. Any artiste who has not auditioned for the agency or 'been seen' in a performance must attend this year's audition to secure their place on the books.

PHOTOS & CV

Please supply no less than ten photographs or Z cards and ten copies of your CV.

THE DATABASE

Please complete and return the database mandate for our computer system. Every artiste has a specific file designed to create a speedy casting service. It is vital that the information supplied is accurate and you keep us updated on your whereabouts, image and of course recent experience.

AGENCY AGREEMENT

On joining the agency all artistes must comply with the terms above and requirements for promotional material. The agency makes no charges other than the commission agreed when you work, except for references, invoice copies or for entries into the casting book and website for your personal promotion.

I have read and understood all the information sent to me and I agree to abide by the terms & conditions of the agency.

Signed: _____

Date:

Points to remember

- Don't rely on agents to find you all your work.
- Agents are not your employers – you are self-employed.
- Arrange to pop in to see your agent from time to time.
- Check in regularly with your agent.
- Choose the right agencies to suit your needs.
- Respect the agency terms and conditions.
- Always write down your audition details when your agent calls.
- Be polite and positive in your agency interview.
- Tell your agent about any other agencies you belong to.
- Build a relationship with your agent.
- Book out when you are not available.
- Never pay to join an agency.
- Telephone your agent after you have been selected from an audition.
- Make sure you know all the details of a job.
- Remember to deduct commission from the total fee.

Chapter Four

Auditions

What is an audition?

An audition is a chance to get work. They will play a large part in your career as it is rare for a dancer to obtain employment without first proving she is the right person for the job. The pressure of trying to get work and coping with audition nerves can prove stressful so it is essential you are ready. The thought of hundreds of dancers in full make-up and heels, brimming at the door of a hot sweaty dance studio trying to get one of the five vacancies available on a contract is enough to make any new dancer give up! The competition is immense. You may be recalled two or three times to an audition before clients reach a decision, depending on the nature of the job. Young hopefuls should be left under no illusions – getting work is tough, but finding your own winning formula to apply to auditions and being prepared will give you an advantage.

Most dancing auditions have roughly the same format, but vary depending on the type of job. Auditions for musicals are probably the most complex, while those for television commercials are quite basic; theatre auditions may contain more than just dancing while a casting may not require you to dance at all.

There are many ways of finding out about auditions. They are always announced with a brief attached, whether it comes via an agent or an advert in the paper as this avoids time-wasting. There are also some adverts which should be avoided. The following diagrams show examples of audition adverts and what to expect from them.

This advert is clear to read without diverting your attention or using enticing or 'cheesy' wording. It gets straight to the point and only gives specific details relevant to the audition. These are all the details you need for now. If you are interested and like the sound of the job, go along to the audition to find out more about the contract. You will get to know the rest after the audition if you are successful.

TWINKLETOES
PRODUCTIONS

FOR 3-MONTH CONTRACT
STARTING MAY 2000
AT
THE ROYAL ALBERT HALL
**MALE AND FEMALE
DANCERS**
Min height 5' 6"

AUDITION
Saturday 16th April 10.00AM
Dance Attic Studios,
368 North End Rd, SW6
Please bring tap shoes & heels.

No calls please

Audition notice 1

(1) It tells you the company who are advertising for dancers, should you wish to do some research before applying.
(2) It tells you the exact venue and length of the contract.
(3) It specifies male and female dancers and the minimum height acceptable.
(4) It gives clear audition details stating date and time at a well-known studio.
(5) It suggests the style of dancing by asking you to bring the relevant footwear. You are asked to bring along tap shoes and heels, so make sure you are a strong tapper and confident dancing in heeled dance shoes.
(6) It specifically asks you not to telephone prior to the audition. They don't wish to be inundated with callers who can't make the audition but want the job, or general time-wasters. The only address given is the audition address, therefore it is pointless telephoning as you will not get through to the client or choreographer, only the studio hired.

GIRL DANCERS WANTED!
FOR BRAND NEW VENUE

'BOMBSHELLS!'

DRESSED AND TOPLESS DANCERS
no consummation
Applicants should be pretty and 18 years or over

AN OPPORTUNITY FOR TERRIFIC EARNINGS!

Please telephone 666 666 666
for an audition time.
Or reply to
P.O. Box 666
enclosing a recent photograph

Audition notice 2

This advert is not as easy to understand. It may be completely innocent, but it is worth knowing how to read into adverts. Some say one thing but mean another. This advert sounds straightforward enough, but is vague in areas and avoids giving specific details.

(1) The heading asks for girl dancers. This may mean they have already got their boys, but it suggests they don't *want* boys. It gives the impression that they just want girls to dance for a male audience.

(2) 'For brand new venue' *could* mean a plush new theatre restaurant in London about to host an exciting floorshow, but it doesn't state the type of venue or where it is. It could be overseas.

(3) 'Bombshells'. The title doesn't sound like a theatre restaurant, but more like a club. It also suggests sexy dancing.

(4) 'Dressed and Topless Dancers'. They are asking for both,

which means if you don't want to dance topless you can be contracted as a dressed dancer. Make sure you apply for the right job and check out all the details. You may be persuaded to join in the finale topless. If you are not comfortable with dancing topless or working with topless dancers think about it before you get involved.

(5) 'No consummation' – this means you are contracted purely as a dancer (always look out for small print on adverts). Consummation means you will be asked to sit at tables with the customers as well as dance in a show. It is a form of hostess work, the idea being that you make the club look busy and give it a glamorous image. You are also encouraged to make conversation with the customers and flirt with them to get them to spend money. Sometimes the customer pays a fee to the club to choose who he sits with. This is not dancing and every dancer should be aware of the meaning of the word consummation before leaping into a contract, especially overseas. (Equity don't approve contracts with consummation.)

(6) It suggests the possibility of good pay. It is probably a low starting wage with an opportunity to top up your earnings by doing more hours or further performances (possibly something you don't wish to do). This vague wording sounds suspicious and could be a loss-leader. If you get the job, investigate the payment terms thoroughly.

(7) Beware of telephoning for separate audition times. Don't be interviewed over the telephone or give away any details just in case. Ask for the full auditioning conditions. Will you be 'seen' with other dancers? If telephone numbers are given in adverts instead of audition times and dates, you are free to call up and ask as many questions about the job as possible. When the wording is not clear it is a good idea to write down a list of questions to find out more about the job before going any further.

(8) A P.O. Box number with no company name is also suspicious. Why have they just asked for a photograph and not a CV? Do they just want good-looking girls with no experience or do they want trained dancers?

(9) This advert has avoided giving important details like: where the job is, how long it's for, the company it's for and the type of dancing required.

What to expect at an audition

The 'open' audition

An 'open' audition basically means the door is open to anyone who would like to audition. These can be tedious as they usually pull in hundreds of hopefuls, a lot of whom won't know the first thing about auditions and are simply trying their luck. An advert will be placed in *The Stage* newspaper with details of the job vacancy and the type of dancers they are looking for. Some jobs have height restrictions; this is for a reason and not just to be unkind to small dancers. It is usually because you will have to fit into particular costumes or match up with existing dancers or celebrities (short celebrities won't use dancers who tower over them). If the minimum height specified is 5' 7" and you are a slim 5' 6" with long legs and a short body you should be able to pass, but if you are 5' 5" and look it you will be wasting your time. Take note and obey instructions.

Auditions are normally held in a rehearsal room or dance studio. It is usually hectic, with dancers getting ready, chatting to friends and warming up before the audition starts. There may be a panel of judges at the audition or just one client, depending on the size of the production. A choreographer will be appointed to run it and will advise the client on the dancers that, in his opinion, interpret the music and dance his routine the best, paying special attention to the detail of his style. Choreographers are artistes, proud of their work, and they want to see their vision come to life by getting you to perform it. The client, on the other hand, is often more concerned with the look of the dancers, especially if they are being used to sell or promote a product. An announcement is given at the beginning of an audition to remind you why you are there and to give you more details about the job you are trying to get.

Audition routines are taught in counts of eight, then demonstrated, repeated several times and set to music. Some choreographers work at a faster pace than others and you should be on your guard. When hundreds of dancers are all lined up like cattle with no room to move or see what the choreographer is setting, it is difficult to pick up the steps. No surprise then that auditions like this are usually nicknamed 'cattle markets'. A caring choreographer will always rotate the dancers so those stuck at the back get a chance to come to the front and see what they've missed. If it is really packed they may send some dancers away and do a second audition at a later date. Once the routine has been taught and is approximately one minute long, you will get a chance to practise it on your own for five minutes. If you can learn it quickly you can then concentrate on your performance. It is also an opportunity for the audition panel to observe the crowd and see who stands out as being the right look for the part (first impressions count). The panel may whisper and point which can be terribly off-putting for a nervous dancer trying to remember her steps.

Names or numbers are called out and you will be placed into groups of four or six; any more than this and it is hard to see the individuals perform. The groups may have to perform several times depending on how quickly the clients reach a decision. This is your chance to smile and display charisma while remembering the routine, staying in time with the music and being watched by the other dancers in the room. It is an ordeal, but it is also part of your profession. It is your chance of employment. The length of auditions vary and usually by the time you have performed in groups for the second or third time the choreographer will pick you by a process of elimination. This is the most difficult part of the day. They usually point at two or three dancers from a group of six and say 'You, you, and you stay, the rest of you thank you very much you can go'. Finally the successful candidates will be asked to dance together once more, then line up for the final choice.

The 'private' audition

A 'private' or 'closed' audition means you have been officially invited to attend by a phone call or a letter. It also means that you have been specifically picked for what you have to offer, whether it is your looks or dancing ability. If a client has asked to see only female dancers with blonde hair who can do excellent tap, then 30 girls who all suit the given brief will be invited to attend a private audition instead of a possible 60 girls attending with the wrong statistics. This usually happens via the filter of an agent who will recommend suitable dancers to his client and saves time for everyone involved.

Private auditions generally start on time and it is most unprofessional to miss the audition or be late (unlike open auditions where it is relatively easy to turn up late and sneak in unnoticed). A register will normally be taken and any gatecrashers will be quizzed about how they came to be there and may be asked to leave. Once the audition is underway the format is much the same as an open audition, the difference being that they are less crowded and the standard of dancing is usually higher. This doesn't make the competition any easier but ensures you are seen properly, increasing your chances, and are not crushed in the stampede of a busy open audition. It is always better to try and get a private audition, especially for musicals, however you first need to write a letter to the relevant client or have an agent to recommend you.

The theatre audition

These auditions are normally held in the theatre where the production will take place, although if the show is going on tour or is being cast outside the city where it will be shown (this is often the case with Pantomimes and Summer Shows), then large rehearsal rooms and studios will house the auditions. Theatre auditions have a different atmosphere and give you a good sense of what the show will actually be like. You enter the audition via the stage door and there is an authentic smell of the previous night's performance. It can be exhilarating, as suddenly you are auditioning in a huge venue, often under stage lights, and are looking out into the darkness of the auditorium and awaiting instructions from a panel sitting hidden in the stalls (we have all seen the films that dramatise these situations!).

Initially you will be asked to dance, as for the other auditions, then if you get through the dance section you are invited to stay and sing. Depending on the musical, you may be asked to sing two contrasting songs to suit the style of the show. Whatever you choose to sing must be supplied on sheet music for the audition pianist and you will be given a brief moment to talk through the tempo/key and feel of your music. You may sing acappella if you prefer. There are lots of people to be heard at these auditions and you may only get a chance to sing part of your song. Some people predict how well they have done by how far through the song they got; if you finished it they must have liked you, if you didn't reach the first chorus you must have been awful. This may not be the case. They have seen hundreds of people and they have got to see hundreds more before the day ends and they may just be in a hurry. Try and choose interesting audition pieces that not only suit your personality, but show your ability. Unless you've been asked to prepare a particular number from the show, don't choose the obvious ones. The directors have heard *Big Spender* again and again and Shirley Bassey does it far better!

The casting

These are normally held at a casting suite and are used primarily for photographic, television and film work. Dancers are not usually required to dance at a casting; they are mainly geared towards choosing people for their looks and are held at locations far too restrictive to dance. Some castings do require you to dance, but this is likely to be unchoreographed 'free style' and if you don't like improvising, beware. A fast-food chain might be casting for dancing gherkins for their latest commercial and they may ask you to act this out.

You will be asked to complete a form on your arrival, answering basic questions and giving details such as availability, previous experience and contact address. You will be told to stand in a particular spot in front of the camera and asked a series of questions which will be answered to camera. This feels uncomfortable as you are listening to the casting director but mustn't make eye contact with him – you must talk to the camera. The questions are always very straightforward, for example:

- what is your name?
- who is your agent?
- where are you from?
- how tall are you?
- can you ride a bike?
- are you available to work on the 27th?
- show me your profile
- pretend you are a dancing gherkin . . .

Castings are generally very quick (apart from the waiting to go in), so bear in mind that you may leave them feeling like you gave an inadequate performance because it happened so fast you didn't get a chance.

All castings for television and film are recorded and taken away to be looked at by the many people involved in making the decisions – the client, producer, director, advertising agency, etc. Tapes are often sent abroad and you won't find out if you've been successful until days later. If you are not successful you won't hear at all unless your agent makes a special call, but casting directors are busy people and hate to be pestered. If faces are being chosen for advertising campaigns then they have to choose the right one.

Preparing for an audition

Preparation is everything if you are to get noticed at an audition. The five minutes you are given to perform could mean professional work for five days or more. It is no use relying on good luck to get you auditions – you need to plan how you will execute each one you attend and that means preparation.

Image

Start by answering the following questions:

- how do you look?
- are you healthy?
- are you overweight?
- are you underweight?
- is your hair in good condition?
- what colours suit your skin and hair colour?
- do you wear any make-up?
- do you wear too much make-up?
- does your audition outfit stand out?
- does it suit your body?
- can you dance with your hair down?
- should you tie it back?

You must decide on the image you want to portray, discover what suits you and go about finding the right clothing. First impressions count and the dancer stood in the corner wearing an ill-fitting leotard and tights with uncombed hair will go unnoticed or be ruled out altogether. If you have bright orange hair it's not a good idea to wear a bright orange outfit as this will appear very 'over the top'. Natural colours are also worth avoiding for the majority of auditions as harsh studio lighting will make you look washed out or naked. Choose colours that complement your hair and skin tone. Dancers love to wear black to look as thin as possible, and if you choose to do this find a style which is different and will be noticed, or introduce another colour to add to it. Dancers dressed in black from head to toe look dreary and pale and you can guarantee that several other dancers will look the same as you. High-street stores sell lots of lycra items nowadays and you don't need to go to a specialist dance shop for leotards and tights. Dancers wear all types of clothes to auditions, anything from the original lycra leotard to combat trousers and bikini tops! There is no set uniform unless otherwise stated in your brief, but you must be able to move in what you wear and it mustn't be so baggy that your body lines can't be distinguished. When dancers tie jumpers around their waists it is not only untidy and annoying to choreographers, but it will be assumed that you have a large bottom!

According to the type of audition you are called for, use your common sense when choosing your outfit, especially for footwear. Commercial dancers are usually very trendy people and can get carried away, taking fashion statements to the limit for a special audition. Before you put on your punk bondage trousers and buffalo platforms, make sure the routine you'll be dancing is simple and that your look suits the type of job. You should eventually try to build a wardrobe of audition gear. The winning red catsuit that helped you get the *Smash Hits* tour may not do the same trick for the *Phantom of the Opera* audition, while if you are auditioning for period dramas then you may want to go for the pale washed out look and leave your red lipstick at home. You have to learn what suits you. Your waif-like best friend might look great in her white satin hot pants, but unless your cheeks stay neatly tucked into a pair too, don't torture yourself by trying to squeeze into the same outfit. Let your body tell you what works. Everyone hates a part of themselves and everyone likes something about themselves. Emphasise your good parts and disguise the bad!

Hair and make-up are equally important for auditions. If you wake up with a huge boil on your chin and it's the day of your face-soap casting, then unless you can do a successful job of covering it up, phone your agent and cancel. The point of the casting is to find someone with flawless skin to sell skincare products. If your skin is usually perfect and you feel that you would normally be the right person for the job, then talk to your agent. They may get you an alternative casting for a day when your skin has had time to heal. Otherwise devote the time to another area of your career and let this one go. Think about the job you are auditioning for before you get ready. If it is a backing tour for Tina Turner, leave your wig at home; if it is a chorus line job, don't be too extravagant as you will have to match with other girls; if you are auditioning for a job with manic choreography, make sure you can see through your hair when you dance. The make-up you choose should be slightly bolder than your everyday make-up. Full stage make-up is not necessary, however, as most auditions are held in natural daylight. Wear brighter make-up to suit a glitzy image and natural colours to suit television castings. Make sure you emphasise cheek bones and lips and highlight eyes, but remember that too much dark make-up will make you look like you've gone ten rounds with Mike Tyson after sweating in a hectic audition.

Attitude

You don't have to be the coolest person in town, but your attitude will account for 50 per cent of your performance at auditions; the other 50 per cent is how you look and react on the outside. You have to control your nerves, keep focused and *think* about what you are doing. Finding a formula to apply to auditions takes time – you need experience to find out what works and what doesn't. I can tell you how to be prepared, but the best way to learn is to jump in the deep end and start auditioning. *If you don't go, you won't know!*

You have to be professional from the start. When you arrive at your audition and join the end of the queue, keep your sanity and stay strong. If you spot the elastic-limbed dancer sitting in box-splits as she puts on her make-up, don't worry; she is confident but she may not be the right person for the job. Don't jump to conclusions. Inside the audition studio you nearly always see a few dancers who know the choreographer and charge up to him to give him a big hug and 'luvvie' kiss, and exchange information about their last job together and the production he is casting that day. Your heart sinks and you wonder: 'why am I bothering – he obviously knows who he wants'. This is sometimes true, and in extreme circumstances an audition is held purely as a publicity stunt. Generally speaking, if a choreographer knows dancers at the audition and has used them before, he may like to use them again if they worked well. However, choreographers like new faces too and need to introduce fresh blood on a regular basis. Remember that it is also the client's decision and he won't have favourites. Just stick with it – you never know what will happen during the audition…

A positive attitude is the secret to success. If you can stay positive, your personality will shine through and you will give out relaxed vibes which will be welcomed by your audience.

People enjoy feeling relaxed. If you watch a comedian on stage who tells his jokes sheepishly and shows signs of being nervous, the audience begin to feel on edge. They may feel sorry for the poor guy on stage or begrudge him for having paid out for a ticket to watch him. Either way the atmosphere is tense. It is the same for any kind of performer, they have to convince their audience they are in control even if they are not.

Controlling nerves is not easy and you have to find a way of recognising them and dealing with them. It is an awful feeling to be raring to go at an audition when suddenly nerves set in and begin to rule your body language. Your muscles twitch, your palms sweat and your mind becomes fuzzy, then you panic because you are no longer in control. As you become more experienced you will recognise these signs and train yourself to channel your nerves into energy. You will eventually learn to ride on nervous energy and spark at auditions. If you look great and feel great then all you need to do is work hard. A confident and happy dancer is on her way to be a working one!

Ability

Your ability stems from your training and previous experience. By answering the following questions you will find out how positive you feel and whether or not you are ready for action. If the answers are 'no', 'I can't remember' or 'I don't know' then consider making some changes before you dive in head first:

- When did you last dance?
- When did you last do a class?
- Have you had full-time training?
- Are your muscles loose?
- Is your physique toned?

- Can you concentrate under pressure?
- Can you pick up routines quickly?
- Can you count in time to the music?
- Are you a versatile dancer or do you stick to one style?

If you have trained to become a professional dancer, your skills, combined with the advice on image and attitude, should give you the ability to start getting professional work. Know your limits and attend only those auditions that suit you. If you are out of your depth you will be wasting your time. Unless you are a classically trained dancer don't expect to be cast in *The Nutcracker*; if you can't rollerskate then don't expect to be cast in *Starlight Express*; and if you are only 5' 2" don't expect to land a casino show in Monaco. Know your capabilities. You can improve your ability by learning a new skill, but you cannot change what your parents gave you.

A dancer's body is her tool and needs constant care and maintenance (see 'health and diet'). You must look after yourself to enable your body to work well. This doesn't mean you have to have a facial every week, but you must pay special attention to your muscles. If you ignore an injury the problem will deteriorate until it gets too bad for you to be able to work and that is the biggest problem of all.

A dancer's bag

Dancers are renowned for carrying huge bags filled with everything but the kitchen sink. My ballet mistress used to recommend a rucksack to be worn over both shoulders to distribute the weight evenly and help to maintain your posture. However you wear your bag, it will always be full of the many items you need for work.

- Diary, pen and pencil.
- Mobile phone or pager.
- Purse or wallet (change for lockers, pay phones, meters).
- A–Z or local street map.
- House keys.
- Photograph and CV.
- Rehearsal gear (sweatpants, trainers).

- Audition gear (outfit for last-minute auditions).
- Wash bag.
- Spot cover-up or loose powder.
- Make-up.
- Hair accessories or a hat.
- Deodorant.
- Jock strap or support bra.
- Knee pads.
- Heels (girls).
- Dance shoes (pointe shoes, tap shoes, jazz shoes, trainers).
- Personal stereo (for rehearsing on the train).
- Energy food (bananas, nuts, bread).
- Energy drink (you may need to skip a meal).
- Dance tights.
- Support bandage and plasters (for injuries).
- *High Kicks.*

Getting chosen at an audition

Not only do you have to physically be seen amongst the crowds, but you need to stand out from the rest. This doesn't mean that you should turn up wearing a Mr Blobby outfit. The way to get spotted is to emphasise your strong qualities and disguise your worst ones. Where you stand is also important, as the dancer who hides in the corner will barely be noticed. Find a spot where you can be seen, remembering to get to the front at some point if the choreographer doesn't ask you to swap around. The best dancers are not always picked during auditions, but then neither are the ones who fling themselves at clients, barge to the front and invade everybody's space. Clients are looking for all kinds of dancer. It may be the person dancing out of time who gets chosen because the director likes her look. Audition technique will develop with experience. You must have faith and always tell yourself that deep down you have that little something that the client is looking for!

After the audition

The recall

You will be asked back on a recall if you were chosen from the initial audition as part of a short list. This may be held on the same day but is more likely to be a few days later. Clients and choreographers recall for any number of reasons:

- to see you audition again because they were unable to decide whether you were right for the job
- they want to give you a second chance – you were awful, but they liked you
- to confirm their decision and see your brilliant performance again
- to get to know you in more detail
- to see how you react on a different day
- to introduce you to other members of the cast or production team
- to match you up with other dancers or costumes.

You will have to go through the whole audition procedure again but in more detail. This time the choreographer will take longer over each part of the audition. The routines may become more complex and you may have to learn set choreography from the show or do two or three different styles of dance. You may also have to read from a script or prepare a speech. It is a good idea to choose some audition pieces that you can work on and learn inside out especially for these occasions. Wear the same clothes to a recall as to the first audition; this way you will be remembered and the panel will have more confidence in you because their memories have been refreshed. Only a select few will be recalled and the auditioning panel will be getting to know you and pay you far more attention, as you are their potential cast. Just remember that it is all good experience and you must have something to offer if they have recalled you. Even if you don't land this job, you have climbed a rung on your career ladder by getting this far and making contact with this particular company who may well offer you a contract in the future. Each time you are called back you will be nearer and nearer to employment and each time you audition you will be stronger and more confident, taking your performance to the next level.

At your final recall they will probably tell you if you will be offered a contract or not, or they may wait a few days and then inform your agent. Only when they have chosen who they want will they reveal the details of the terms of the contract and the salary on offer. After going to great lengths to get the job you can only hope your agent can negotiate the contract to suit you!

A provisional booking

A provisional booking usually refers to a job for which they wish to book you providing the job actually takes place. It means you are the person they wish to use depending on a number of circumstances that must fall into place first. For example, the weather (for filming), matching you up to other cast members, arranging the technical team and location, the time in which they have to do the project and the budget available to cover everything. So much of the industry depends on other people, and dancers are often the last link in the chain. They offer you a provisional booking to stop you taking alternative work should they wish to use you, but if the job falls through they can drop you straight away without being tied to a contract or confirmed booking – they don't owe you a penny. However, provisional bookings are usually confirmed 24 hours prior to the job itself, if not sooner, and you are well within your rights to take something else if it hasn't been confirmed by then, but check with your agent's or union conditions.

A provisional booking might be organised as follows. A record company asks their marketing department to do a promotional video for an artiste's forthcoming single. A video company is appointed who create a storyboard or 'treatment' which in this case will involve a cast of dancers. The video company appoint a director who appoints a casting director who phones a selection of agents who supply dancers for an audition. Five dancers are chosen at the audition and are *provisionally* booked for a day's filming on Monday. This is only the beginning. Before those dancers make it on to the set any one of the following factors could result in the provisional booking being cancelled:

- the director only likes four out of the five provisionally booked dancers – one gets dropped
- the agent negotiates a fee which will only pay for three dancers – two get dropped
- the location is unavailable on Monday so the shoot changes to Tuesday – three dancers are unavailable
- the record company cuts the budget – four dancers get dropped
- the artiste hates the storyboard so it changes at the last minute – all dancers get dropped.

Of course it works both ways and sometimes you are provisionally booked for a job which has many potential spin-offs and you are faced with a diary full of confirmed bookings.

Being 'pencilled'

Being pencilled is similar to being provisionally booked – a client would like you to write in your diary (in pencil) a day on which he would like you to be available to work should he need you. However, until you are confirmed you can still accept any other definite bookings. A pencilling usually refers to a job on which a decision cannot be reached by all of the production team as to which dancer they wish to book, therefore, three or four dancers will be placed 'on pencil' until they can make up their mind. Then they may give two dancers a 'heavy pencil' until eventually one dancer will be confirmed. Being pencilled usually occurs in television and film work where scripts and arrangements are subject to change so often that they have to be vague about the final cast and put off confirmation and contracts for as long as possible.

'On stand by'

Being 'on stand by' is self-explanatory and is used as a precaution when a dancer has been confirmed, but an extra dancer is booked to be 'on stand by' in case of injuries or problems occurring during the contract. Whether the dancer is on site or on call at home, she must be paid for her time even if she doesn't perform. It is an added cost for production companies and unless it is a long contract they will not book a stand-by dancer, although theatre shows have 'swings' and understudies (see 'Musicals').

Coping with rejection

You have travelled some distance to attend a long-awaited audition on which you have pinned all your hopes for a job for the summer; you have spent hours working your guts out and got yourself to the final line of eight dancers, when they decide to take six blondes – and you have dark hair. It's just not your lucky day! It may be that you didn't show off your best qualities or you barely got noticed. Whatever the reason for your lack of success, you have to accept it and deal with your disappointment. Tell yourself again and again: 'there will be other auditions for better jobs', 'I didn't get the job because something better is around the corner', 'it is their loss that they didn't choose me'. Keep thinking positively, give the audition a quick post mortem in your head or with a friend and then forget it. The worst thing you can do is mull it over for days on end, working yourself into a stupor and becoming frustrated and bitter. This will reflect in your personality. Avoid anxiety and find a way to relax by doing something you enjoy that is nothing to do with your work, then try to let it go and look forward to the next part of your career. This is not easy when you are disappointed and feel depressed, but as you become more experienced you will realise that something else always comes along.

If you failed at your audition because you didn't reach the standard required then you should go away and work on that weakness. If you *keep* failing at auditions, you need to take a step back and try and discover where you are going wrong. Think of a plan to iron out the problems that may be losing you the jobs and try adapting a slightly new method to your next audition. If you left the audition feeling that you really did your best and couldn't have done any better, then be proud of your efforts and try and focus on the good moments you experienced. You have just met new people, you have made new contacts and you have done a physical workout. Unfortunately you didn't get the job, but you have gained important experience. Everyone is entitled to good and bad days at work. Your career is a building process – it will not be make or break in a day. Think about the long-term prospects and above all keep positive.

Points to remember

- Don't be late – you will feel stressed and unprepared, especially if you miss the start of the audition.
- Space yourself as well as possible. Don't position yourself too close to someone else or stand in a row.
- Be confident. Auditions can fill you with endless insecurities; shut them out the minute they creep into your head and concentrate on giving your best.
- Pay attention and keep quiet – choreographers need to concentrate and you may miss an important point if you are busy chatting. Wait until afterwards to gossip with friends.
- If the routine looks too difficult for you, don't leave or panic. They may be testing you on purpose. Try and stay calm and see it through to the end – you never know what they will be expecting of you.
- Pace yourself. If the routine is taxing, don't dance flat out when you are learning the routine. Save your energy and don't get too sweaty until you have to.
- Watch yourself in the mirror while learning the audition routine, but always make eye contact with the judging panel and perform to them when you finally dance.
- Keep focused on your own work – don't lose faith in yourself and copy another dancer's counts at the last moment. You are probably right and she is wrong.
- If you forget the choreography, keep moving and improvise until you can pick it up again. You would be expected to do this in a performance, so show you can do it now. It might land you the job!
- Don't be too cheeky or chatty with clients – be diplomatic and polite.
- Your best performance is enough, so aim for it every time!

Part Two

Working As A Dancer

Now you have trained and are ready to find work as a dancer, you need to investigate the options and find the type of work that suits you best. There is a wide spectrum of commercial dancing jobs to consider, and so much to cover that you don't have time to get bored. Even when you're not working, you have the challenge of finding out about forthcoming productions, making new contacts and going to auditions every day. You may have trained with a specific type of job in mind; many dancers train in musical theatre in the hope that they will one day perform in a West End production. However, you may find your chosen type of work doesn't suit you at all and it would be better for you to go in a different direction.

This section outlines the different types of commercial dance work available and includes advice from experienced dancers and profiles influential choreographers. It also covers other areas you may consider exploring to further your career. Whether you want to dance on a Caribbean cruise, in a Paris show palace, on television or in Wembley Stadium, it will explain what each job involves and what is expected of a professional dancer.

Chapter Five

Television

The television dancer

Dancing on television is a popular choice as an aspect of a dancer's career, but the reality is that only a limited number actually get the opportunity. Television dancing covers game shows, variety shows, award shows, pop shows, children's television, documentaries, films and dramas. There are few television dancing jobs now compared to the wide variety back in the 70s, but if a dancer gets to do at least one TV job it sits very nicely on her CV.

The television shows that regularly feature dancers are very popular and very well done. Production companies are commissioned by the major TV channels to make the shows, but technology has grown so fast that game shows are computerised and commercialised to such an extent that it is no longer necessary to use dancers to pad out the show and make time for adding up scores. Comedy and variety shows on the other hand are full of old pros and you may find yourself doing more than dancing by acting in sketches or assisting the host. There are many ways to broaden your career options once you have got your foot in the door of television and observed how it all works. If you're fortunate you may find yourself on a dancing show that has a second series. If the first series is successful they may keep the same image for subsequent ones. However, they may wish to change faces and use different dancers each time.

Open auditions are rarely held for TV shows; they tend to ask a well-known choreographer for recommendations. They don't have time to analyse showreels or try out new choreographers, and it is therefore the existing choreographer's task to find reliable dancers. He may decide to organise an audition via the dance agencies, or he may telephone dancers who he knows could handle the job, direct. If you're lucky enough to get a television dancing job you will be contracted for rehearsals and filming days. If your contract is not issued by Equity, make sure it has been 'Equity approved'. Your agent should be able to look over it and advise you on this. But if you are at all unsure fax a copy to Equity to have it checked. This way you will receive all monies due to you for your performance. For example, repeats may be shown and you should receive a percentage of your original fee every time, likewise if a video is made out of footage you've appeared in. It is sensible to have an agent to guide you; don't run into signing your rights away at the excitement of getting TV work.

Although TV work is thought of as a credible job and sounds good, the reality can be quite demanding. Unlike dancing on stage, where you have a set time to rehearse and a set time to perform, TV is very 'stop' and 'start'. There is a lot of hanging around waiting for technical things to be done, and when you are dancing on the set you need to be able to coordinate many things at the same time as concentrating on your routine. For example, camera angles may suddenly change and you will need to adapt. There will be up to four different cameras filming you, from above, below, behind or close up front, and when the red light is shining, it's switched on! You will particularly have to watch out for the 'steadicam' – a cameraman running about holding his camera, closely followed by an assistant guiding him and getting the wires out of the way. The idea is to get abstract shots of dancing feet or spontaneous action. The set is often an odd-shape, with no back or front and limited space, leaving 12 dancers to look as polished and energetic as possible when they are virtually dancing on the spot and trying not to get too disorientated every time they double pirouette.

TV studios can be vast places and you must make sure you know where you are supposed to be and who with, or you may find yourself wandering on to the *EastEnders* set when you should be doing *Top Of The Pops*! There are also huge numbers of crew and production staff on TV shows. Report to the floor manager or the assistant director, but don't ask the director a question unless he is talking to you; his head is full of the whole production and he may unintentionally treat you unkindly. To him everyone is like a piece of a jigsaw he needs to put in place.

Filming can be long and tedious. You spend five hours sitting in the coffee bar, and are then called on to the set for a two-minute rehearsal before doing a take. Having said that, there is normally a good atmosphere, especially in front of a live audience, and when you are sat at home six weeks later and all your family and friends see you appear on TV it is something to be proud of.

Pan's People, 1973

Period films and dramas

Dancers of all ages are used to reproduce historical ballroom scenes, country and tea dances, and so on, in period films and dramas. Television companies go to great lengths to create authenticity in a period production and they will cast their dancers as meticulously as the principal actors to get the correct looks, so being a Jane Austen lookalike is not such a bad thing! They will employ a suitable choreographer who specialises in that particular era to recreate the look. Filming is usually on location, often in the part of the world in which the original story was set.

Films are different to television shows as the filming is more sporadic and often done back to front. You may rehearse with the director and actors in August and not film until October because the cast have to go and film scenes in India, and you may do the final wedding dance scene before the marriage. The work is nearly always spread out over time and your contract will bind you accordingly. You will have to do all the dates or none at all, as if you pull out before the filming is complete you will ruin their continuity. Working in films may also involve dancing with an actor who has to film dialogue during a dance, and this means you have to dance in silence, without music. How does everyone keep in time? You will be given a flesh-coloured in-ear monitor to wear which will play the music directly into one ear. This can be off-putting and awkward to wear, especially if you have a temperamental one that only plays sections of the music and throws you out of time, but it is a clever idea and solves all the sound technician's problems.

Dance costumes in period productions are a novelty and trying on the relevant attire of the era is great fun, but five days on a freezing cold location when you can't feel your toes and have to dance wearing a corset and lots of heavy petticoats doesn't do wonders for a glamorous dancer's image! You really do go back in time and experience the discomforts of corsets and lack of central heating. Make-up and hair is also a lengthy process and it can be an early morning call into make-up if there are lots of dancers and extras to do. If the director needs you on set by 9a.m. you could be called in up to three hours earlier to get ready. The comforting thoughts are good pay and another diamond on the CV. Catering on film sets is also a big bonus – all bought and paid for and pre-pared beautifully: cooked breakfast, tea breaks, lunch, more tea breaks, dinner, and if filming goes on late (nearly always) then supper too! Dancers on strict diets, be warned!

Television commercials

Like actors, models, children and animals, dancers are used to sell products in TV commercial breaks. You may remember the rubber dancing man in the Guinness commercial, or the Halifax commercial in which a house was built out of dancing and somer-saulting people. An advertising agency will come up with an idea to present to their client, and from there a storyboard is put together, followed by a casting to which dancers are invited to audition for the job via their agents.

Commercials usually involve a one- or two-day shoot and can take you to foreign locations for some products. As with most filming, days are long, but adverts never drag on and are shot, cut and edited speedily, and usually transmitted within a few weeks. There may be more than one featured artiste in a commercial; you can be very highly paid for a featured part and receive an adequate fee for being a background artiste. Television commercial royalties are very confusing to understand and it is wise to have an agent to negotiate your deal, especially if it is to be shown worldwide, as you will be due a basic fee followed by a royalty or a 'buy out' fee. Equity issue information booklets on definitions for artistes appearing in commercials (walk-on, background, feature etc.) and explain the current agreements and how commercial fees and repeats operate.

Commercial advertising is a very transient field, and everything may change at the last minute because the advertising company alter the storyboard. It is very much about achieving a 'look' and if it doesn't work often the whole idea is scrapped. Commercial work is almost always booked via your agent, and there are some agencies that specialise in television commercial work, representing a handful of people with feature-friendly faces! I'm sure you've seen familiar faces crop up in various commercials. Well, they have the 'look' for advertising products. You may or may not be one of these faces and you won't find out until you start going to commercial castings. If your face doesn't fit now, try again later; a more mature look may do the trick.

Dancing on a commercial can be quite a novelty as dancers tend to be introduced either to indicate sheer happiness and celebration or to actually be the product. For dancers your face isn't quite as important as your personality and versatility, particularly if you are called upon to be a dancing crisp packet or a lettuce leaf! Choreography is generally simple and jolly: a showgirl kickline to announce the Courts showroom sale, an ordinary couple who start to rock 'n' roll when they have McCain Oven Chips for tea and Captain Birds Eye's ship full of dancing sailors are all examples of dancing adverts. Commercials are generally positive productions full of fun to entice you to buy a product. Advertising is a clever game. It is not only about you looking great, it is about you making the product you're selling look great. If you have the 'look' and are lucky enough to be cast in TV commercials then well done – you have found a good way to subsidise your dancing career.

Chapter Six

Shows

When a show is put together professionally, all the pieces of the jigsaw slot into place to create a spectacular display of lights, scenery, music and action. Dancers feature in musicals, theatre shows (including pantomimes and summer shows), casinos and showbars and are an important element in these types of show, knitting the productions together with their presence of colour, energy and skill. Working in musicals is an excellent achievement and many dancers train on specially designed musical theatre courses with this in mind. Performing in West End theatres to packed audiences every night is very rewarding and makes all the hard work of building a career worthwhile. Travelling abroad and working as a show dancer is a perfect way to see the world while earning a consistent wage and dancing, and then there are the shows back home that cover the winter and summer periods. A dancer who hops between pantomime and summer season has the advantage of guaranteed work for up to eight months of the year, but she must be prepared to move where the work is, which means constantly living in digs away from her home. Whatever the show, it is a fabulous lifestyle and rewarding work for dancers.

Singing as a dancer

A dancer will find there are more options open for her if she can sing as well as dance. If you are primarily a dancer who can sing, you need to be confident and tuneful; if you are a strong all-round performer you will find yourself auditioning for parts in musicals and shows as well as working as a chorus member; if, on the other hand, you are an excellent singer who dances well and looks great, then you can discover the world of recording and the potential benefits of being a pop star. There are many ways to use your singing voice in conjunction with your dancing career.

Confidence plays a large part in whether you believe in your-self as a 'singer' or not. If you trained all your life to be a dancer and you are a casual singer who confines your singing to your own home, then it may take some years before you realise that with a little more confidence you could actually combine the two in a professional job. Most dance colleges provide drama and singing lessons, but they are often not taken seriously enough. These valuable lessons are sometimes skipped and then regretted later on. It's hard to get your career in perspective at the time of training because all you think about is dancing, and students are unaware of how useful other lessons are. There will be a time in your professional career when you think 'if only I could sing or at least have a go', and you can if you think about it early on. There are a handful of us who are tone deaf and wouldn't dream of putting ourselves through the trauma of singing, but there are so many dancers who only lack the confidence, and a small amount of attention on their singing voice will open up more doors in their future career.

Singing is becoming as much of a 'hang up' for dancers as being thin. Once again it is down to the circumstances and who is looking at you. If you can find the guts to make as many mistakes as it takes to make you successful then you will be a winner. Do an audition and sing flat, go to karaoke nights and make a fool of yourself, sing like an injured cat in lesson time and break through the barrier of being afraid to sing. You will get there eventually.

Musicals

If you have trained in musical theatre you may have your mind set on a place in the West End. To land a part in a musical you will need to get through some intensive auditions first. This often proves difficult for dancers who can dance well but lack confidence in their singing. The ensemble in a show has to have strong all-round performers, although they can get away with having a handful of extraordinarily strong dancers with weaker, but in tune singing voices as they can use booth singers off-stage to enhance the sound. If you regularly get through the first round at musical auditions but are then 'kicked out' in the singing round, it may be down to your confidence and nerves on the day or your choice of audition song. Don't attempt a Celine Dion ballad if you sing like Orville the duck. Think about what will suit your voice. A carefully picked audition song can complement your voice enough to get you through the audition, providing you sing and perform with confidence. It is essential to have charisma and personality as no-one will cast a wooden or embarrassed performer.

Musical contracts have the advantage of being at least 12 months long, giving a dancer financial security (unless of course the show is in danger of closing early). Musicals also tour the UK and Europe, and British dancers can be contracted for the majority of these shows. To be able to dance on Broadway, however, you will need a work visa. When a musical goes on the road you will have to change accommodation accordingly. This is usually straightforward and when you sign your contract you will receive an itinerary and a 'digs list' telling you where to find suitable and safe accommodation. You will meet up with other dancers in rehearsals who are in the same position as you, so you can help each other with the touring arrangements. Musicals are large shows so they only change destination about every 6–12 weeks.

Being in a musical is quite a novelty because they are larger than life productions, with lavish sets and costumes and wonderful designs and effects. Musicals recreate anything from a palace to a planet; *Starlight Express* manages to reconstruct an entire railway track around the auditorium, and the dancing is styled to the theme of the show. It is the same with *Cats*; the dancers in the cast have to study the natural moves of a cat, observing how they jump, how they wash and how they prowl. This is reflected in the choreography and the movements are exclusive to the show. Rehearsal periods vary, but are normally at least six weeks for dancers in the ensemble. Attention is paid to every detail of the story and routines are polished to perfection. There is no busking for dancers in musicals, it is 100 per cent effort from day one. Musicals are renowned for their strong casts and fabulous music scores. They don't necessarily have a cast full of celebrities, although initially 'a name' to play the star role helps the show get off the ground and once the production is established it depends on the critics and the show's reputation to bring in the audience. The company cannot therefore afford to have any weak points or employ unsatisfactory artistes. Some musicals have been known to go through a phase of teething problems at the start of their run, but come through them to become smash hit, long-lived productions.

Timing in musical shows is crucial, it must keep the audience interested. Good acting is also important, and this is often a difficult task for dancers as they have non-speaking parts, yet it is still essential they stay in character and are believable in their role. They may be given a line of dialogue to say, which is even harder as you are not a character the audience can warm to and you only have one shot at saying something.

Understudy

If you are a dancer with a strong singing voice you may get the job as understudy to a principal part. An understudy learns the entire role of the part she is covering as well as learning and performing her own chorus role. She needs to be aware of all the stage directions of the part and know the script inside out. This is because anything could happen at the last minute (before or even during a show) and she has to understudy the part and perform for the night. Understudies are essential to all musicals as whole chunks of the story would be missing without the principal cast on stage. Part of an understudy's rehearsal is to watch numerous performances of the part she is covering so she can adapt her own performance in a suitable way. She is not expected to mimic the performer, but to portray the story and give her best as if the part was always hers. A good understudy often ends up playing the part if the original cast member leaves.

David Olton playing Richie in A Chorus Line, UK tour 1997

PHOTO: HUGO GLENDINNING

A swing

A swing is the same sort of role as an understudy, but requires the dancer to learn several parts – not principal roles but the chorus or cameo parts. It is a difficult job as she needs to learn a number of different versions of the stage directions and have the choreography firmly implanted in her memory. If a dancer twists an ankle during a performance, she will need to spring into action and take over the position. A swing does not perform every night, but gets made-up and ready then watches the show from the wings or waits in the dressing room. It can be tedious learning several roles in the show then not performing any of them, but she still gets paid. With a large dancing cast it is inevitable that dancers will be ill, injured or in desperate need of a night off at some point.

Summer season

Summer seasons are designed to provide entertainment for people on holiday. They are very much family-oriented shows and are usually situated in theatres at seaside resorts, the most famous venue being 'the end-of-pier show'. These days they are also likely to be in purpose-built theatres in the heart of a 'Butlins'-style holiday park or maybe an ice show in a theme park. You will be contracted to dance in the show for a specific number of weeks. They can run for six weeks to six months of the summer; the larger shows run for the longest period, usually those starring celebrity names to draw the audiences in.

Over the years there has been a basic format to a summer season show, with various acts appearing on the bill and the most famous of them topping the show. Each act is self-contained and a troupe of dancers perform in-between them. The structure has remained the same, but the acts are now becoming much more interactive with each other and the shows are written, rehearsed and created for a specific season. They are a lot more high-tech as well, with impressive lighting and special effects. The acts are also more imaginative – magicians are no longer making rabbits appear from hats, but are escaping from padlocked chests in a tank of water and dancers are often used throughout the show to assist with the illusions or in comedy sketches.

Summer season dancers have a reputation for wearing silver

sandals and too much make-up, and occasionally appearing tacky or of a poor standard, but this is not necessarily so. The choreography and costumes have moved with the times, and although the shows still appeal to the family audience, this line of work is becoming more commercial and more challenging for dancers. Some shows consist predominately of dancing, with a whole section of the show devoted to different styles of dance, with elaborate costumes and impressive quick changes. If you audition for an established company you can build your whole career around working for them and stay working for years. It is also sometimes a way in to television work, as the show may be so successful that it is televised. You may become part of a sketch with the 'top of the bill' who then gets his own TV series and asks you to appear with him, or the same choreographer may be used for the TV series and he may prefer to keep the same dancers. Anything is possible.

Summer season is great fun. You entertain families who are on holiday for one or two weeks, and end up feeling like you're on holiday yourself! The cast seem to become a family themselves, arranging picnics during the day or going to restaurants after the

Summer season at the Futurist Theatre, Scarborough: 'The City Life Dancers'

show at night. The show itself will often be full of 'in jokes' that apply only to the cast. All this fun and you receive a wage packet at the end of the week (you do not have to wait for money on these jobs). Summer seasons are secure and enjoyable jobs for dancers.

Pantomime

Pantos are generally shows based on fairy tales and presented at Christmas time. They are family shows, designed to be magical and fun for children, and have a wonderful atmosphere as there is a lot of interaction with the audience, all of whom are in a festive mood! It can get quite hectic as there is so much going on and the audience gets very excited.

All kinds of performers appear in pantomime – *Blue Peter* presenters, Gladiators, even heavyweight boxers! The celebrities are given characters to play (a goody, a baddy, a hero etc.) and are usually given the principal parts to help pull in the audiences. The shows are very tongue-in-cheek and although they are full of wonderful effects, they are never Oscar-winning productions. The shows are based around fun and laughter for families, with tons of age-old jokes and songsheets that still bring the house down. The dancers help to tell the story and the routines are based around each part of the fairy tale. Depending on the pantomime the dancers may not dance as much as they would like, and in-between numbers they spend the time standing around as 'villagers'. On the other hand, some pantos keep dancers very busy being a ship's crew or Daisy the cow as well as fitting in lots of routines! The costumes are always great fun in panto because they are straight out of the story books, huge glittery ballgowns and robes or Arabian jewels and pantaloons.

Rehearsals are two or three weeks prior to opening. The show will take shape pretty quickly as it has been done so many times before. Pantomime dancing can be hard work with two perform-ances each day, sometimes virtually back to back, with just enough time to down a sandwich between performances. You will probably end up having a disjointed Christmas, travelling up the motorway on Boxing Day to do a matinée. When Christmas is out of the way, however, you will be one of the few dancers working in January, which is generally the grimmest month to find dancing work. The wages are regular and there are all kinds of bonus wages for performing on Sundays or bank holidays over the Christmas period. Some pantomimes run through Christmas and almost up to Easter! Weekends will be the busiest show times and your day off will be a weekday and of course Christmas Day. Like the summer shows the cast become very close and there is a great working atmosphere, particularly as it is Christmas time!

Showgirls and guys

Show dancing is usually known as 'showgirl work', but male dancers play an equally important role in this type of work. Showgirls and guys are part of glitzy productions seen in casinos, showbars, hotels, theatre-restaurants, show palaces or on cruise liners. You can be employed as a dressed, topless or naked (often with body decoration) show dancer and the type you opt for will be reflected in your wages (the more you reveal, the more you are paid). The shows are very visual and you are admired for wearing the flamboyant, sparkling costumes that light up the stage, and for the syncopated dancing patterns and kicklines you and 29 others perform. Depending on the size and status of the venue, between ten and 100 dancers may be booked for a show of this kind.

Show dancers need excellent posture and elongated limbs. It is a known fact that real show dancers are not under 5ft 7in tall unless they have an extremely lean figure. The necessary qualities for a show dancer are long limbs, height, flexibility and elegance. Tall, classically trained dancers often work as show dancers at some point in their career because they carry these qualities.

Male show dancers are not normally tagged on to the end of a female kickline, but dance their own all-male one. Their attire is just as glitzy, with just as many costume changes, and sometimes they wear only trousers or maybe a tail suit in the same colour and style as the girls' costumes. At a large show palace they also wear body decoration and head-dresses. The guys do exciting partner work and often lift the girl dancers, parading the stage with them sitting on their shoulders. The guys may also be used to incorporate a different angle to the show; perhaps they will do a tap routine or a supporting number with a singer while the girls do a costume change. A popular number is an adagio act. This is where a male and female dancer perform a beautiful *pas de deux* to lyrical music.

Show dancers

As a show dancer you are allowed to go over the top when dressing up, and layer on stage make-up, false eyelashes, feathers, sequins, American tan tights, tassels and large fussy head-dresses! Having said that, these days the costumes are far more abstract and the sets and lighting create spectacular illusions – you may end up dressed like a panther dancing on a rotating jungle set.

When applying for showgirl/guy work read adverts and check contracts carefully. Some hotels and nightclubs may ask you to do consummation or wear costumes you don't approve of. Make sure you do not have to have any contact with the audience or act as a hostess in-between shows. Some jobs invite you to be in a show but want your services in other ways too; sitting at a table looking gorgeous and persuading customers to buy expensive champagne is the usual ploy on these precarious contracts. This is consummation and should be avoided unless you are fully aware of what is expected from you.

Show palaces and casinos

When you hear about casinos and showbars you visualise a world of money and glamour. This is generally true and the venues that put on shows of this nature are usually expensive nights out. Casinos are designed for people to wine, dine and gamble their money away, and in order to entice them into a particular venue the host will create a palace-type welcome of beautiful interiors, a superior dinner menu and champagne list, and inviting tables. To keep you there for the evening he will present his shows two or three times a night for entertainment. Casinos and showbars vary and appeal to different audiences. Some are aimed purely at tourists as part of an authentic night out, most famously in Vegas or Paris, while some are aimed at the rich as their regular evening playtime.

You will work as part of a team and usually make lots of friends, helping to create a happy working environment. The work is night-time only, which leaves the rest of your day to sleep, shop or fit in other work. You will get a fair wage and be contracted six monthly or yearly – that is a lot of dancing work! As a show dancer you must develop the skill of making glamorous and usually uncomfortable and heavy stage costumes move with grace as you unfold beautiful patterns on the stage. You must create an illusion for your audience, while in reality you are squeezed into inhuman bikinis decorated with finery (normally with razor sharp sequin edges digging into your armpit creases), wearing 5in heels and a heavy head-dress with feathers and fruit dangling in your eyes. You must know how to work as a team and glide around the stage smoothly, being fully aware of your dance colleagues and keeping up a glittering grin. You must also perfect your kickline – the dancer on the end trying to be a soloist by kicking her leg over the choreographed 90 degrees will just make it look ugly.

Sun City in South Africa is one of the largest show palaces in the world. The show dancers here are immaculately conditioned to be the exact weight and height required for their outstanding costumes. The shows are amazing and if you don't have what it takes, you don't get to stay. Dancers are weighed regularly and fined if they put on weight!

Cruise ships

Cruise ships are like floating hotels, and the entertainment programme they present is an important part of the voyage. The
guests will gather in a specially designed theatre or the main
ballroom to watch a floorshow, the main evening attraction for
guests after they've had dinner and before they dance the night
away in the discotheque. The shows are compact and fast-moving
and normally contain male and female dancers. They are aimed at
family audiences and often have a theme; for example restaged
excerpts from West End musicals, a Can Can, or dancing through
the years (60s, 70s and 80s) is a favourite, showing lots of partner
work and a variety of dance styles. Dancing on a ship constantly
moving on water is quite a novelty and takes some getting used to
(the types of stage floor vary). Depending on the size of the ship,
between four and ten dancers will be contracted (under half will
be male). As well as the dancers, other self-contained acts will
appear in the show – many contract a singer/dancer who learns
the dance numbers but also sings solo throughout the show and
leads the production numbers, while an adagio act is also a regular
feature. Costumes are created and fitted specially. They are not
usually restricting or too skimpy, but are designed for quick
costume changes, so accessories are often kept to a minimum.

Being a dancer on a cruise ship is an excellent experience and
every young professional should try it. It not only introduces you
to the industry of dancing, but it is a completely different world to
normal life and worth doing before you have too many ties back
home (it is difficult to maintain a relationship because of the
nature of the business). The audience on a cruise are on holiday
and are therefore relaxed and having fun. This creates a wonderful atmosphere for the workers on the ship and it becomes a
working holiday for dancers. Some ships will have no other duties
for you other than dancing in their evening show (and rehearsing
when necessary); the rest of the time will be your own to discover
the countries you dock in. It is an excellent opportunity to travel
and earn a living at the same time. Certain ships may contract you
to do some extra duties, such as hosting activities on deck, calling
the Bingo, or dressing up and welcoming the guests to the
captain's cocktail party. Dancers on ships become very close. You
are in each other's pockets, dancing and travelling together and
usually sharing cabins. It can also be lonely out at sea among

families together on holiday, so having close friends is very important.

Cruise ship contracts are a minimum of 3 months for Scandinavia and the Mediterranean, but the majority are 6–12 months for worldwide or Caribbean cruises. Some dancers work on cruise ships and never get off – it's too much of a good thing. Why should you have to audition at cattle markets day in, day out, and run from casting to casting in the pouring rain? If you have found a comfortable dancing career with one or many cruise line companies you can ship-hop for years, and the longer you stay with a company the more beneficial it becomes. You are allowed to invite your partner or family to visit you on the ship for a nominal fee, you can get away with doing shorter contracts, and eventually you may be promoted to head girl, assistant choreographer or even choreographer for the company!

Chapter Seven

Cabaret

The true meaning of the word cabaret is 'entertainment provided in a restaurant or night-club while the customers are eating'. It therefore includes the wide spectrum of show work I have already covered however I have categorised it separately because, dare I say it, it is a dated title for the spectacular shows seen in showbars. Cabaret work for dancers generally means dancing in a group, or act, in venues that don't house big productions. This does not mean that *they* are dated, however. Cabaret acts and dancers are highly professional people and have done their ground work. Once you have done cabaret you can handle almost anything. The majority of your work as a cabaret dancer will involve travelling around hotels, theatre restaurants, cabaret clubs, working men's clubs, night-clubs, hostess clubs and country clubs, and you normally spend a lot of time on the road between shows (unless of course you get a residency). Some large venues have their own stage just for the cabaret, while at others the cabaret will be performed on the dance floor. Cabaret is fulfilling work for a dancer as it can involve lengthy shows of up to 45 minutes of pure dancing, incorporating quick changes and projecting tremendous energy.

Dance groups

The great thing about being in a dance group is that you can work with your friends as a team, changing the routines whenever you fancy and dancing to music that really inspires you. You are your own boss and can pursue your own ideas. Starting up on your own is a big responsibility and takes a lot of effort. Dance groups are completely self-contained with between three and six dancers, and you do your own choreography, arrange your own rehearsals (in the beginning this may be in your living room until you can afford to book a studio), and choose and record your own music. This must be of excellent quality as it will be played loud in the clubs

and if it distorts it will ruin the performance. The shows should be edited on a good-quality sound system and put on to a DAT or CD (with back-up cassettes) to avoid it getting ruined. You will also have to make sets of costumes for each member of the group. You may have to say goodbye to the first few payments you receive to cover these costs and possibly pay for help from a dressmaker and a sound engineer. This all sounds like hard work but starting your own business or working as part of a team is immensely satisfying and educational.

The group has to build a repertoire that can be performed to different audiences. You would usually include a theme number and a variation of styles into the show – perhaps a 60s feel or a futuristic number? The length of a show varies with each venue. You may be asked to dance two 25-minute shows with three costume changes in each, or you may have to do 30 minutes in one go. The most you will be asked to perform is two 45-minute shows, each with four or five costume changes and different routines, but this is normally in hotels abroad. Forty-five minutes is a lot of dancing and a long time for one dance group to hold an audience, so make sure it remains visually exciting and that you get paid enough for your efforts.

Once you have created your show you need to promote your-selves. This also becomes costly. Cabaret artistes usually use glossy colour photographs and advertise in places like *Showcall* (a directory of cabaret acts) or at the back of *The Stage*. Your CVs are not relevant in getting gigs for the group, but each member should write a short piece about the group and together you can create a biography to include in a press release which can be sent to club owners with your photographs. Eventually you should consider making a showreel with short excerpts of your routines. Clients like to know what they are booking and may insist on seeing your act beforehand. A showreel saves time and is a worthwhile investment in the long term. You will also need to join a few cabaret agents who specialise in club bookings and represent comedians, singers and dancers. They often book out complete shows to venues and welcome a good self-contained dance group.

One member of the group may be in charge of everything while the others do the dancing, or you may share the different jobs between you (costumes, tape editing, mail-outs and so on). Sometimes an ex-dancer turned choreographer runs a group or several dance groups and rotates them in the clubs and contracts them abroad. You will need a strong, catchy name that indicates the type of act you are – off the wall, raunchy, comical? – and to

Dance group 'Hot Club'

keep a date sheet or diary in which to plan your gigs. Avoid double-booking yourself, and if you do accept two gigs on one night remember to allow for travel distance and time. You will have to be organised and keep all your paperwork, contracts and receipts safe to help with your accounting and tax returns.

It may take a few years to establish yourselves and get enough regular work to cover the costs. When solo cabaret acts are booked, there is only one person to be paid, but for a group the payment has to be split between each dancer and cover the cost of petrol to the gigs, costume maintenance etc. The advantages are that once you become established you can get offered some lovely contracts. It is a good way to travel without being away from home for too long because the contracts are generally short (1–4 weeks). You can find work all year round, working at home or abroad, and Christmas time is likely to be the busiest period. You may find yourself on a beach for New Year's Eve because you've been booked to dance at a hotel in Dubai, or you may get sent abroad for a two-week tour entertaining the British troops, or find you are offered a resident position in one club where you can dance in the same venue for a few months without having to go on the road.

On the road

If you are a member of a group touring different venues each night, you will need to be very adaptable and very dedicated. Travelling up and down the country takes hours and you need to do some careful route planning to avoid getting lost or meeting heavy traffic. It can be tiring, especially if you are driving yourselves, and it is wise to share the driving. When I was in a group we would draw straws for the jobs – mend costumes in the back of the car, drive to the gig, or do a solo number in the show!

Touring on the cabaret circuit is the best dancing experience you can gain. You will see so many different environments, with different lighting, floor space, changing facilities and audiences. One night the stage will be tiny, the next night it may be a glass dance floor which you will have trouble standing up on. It will prepare you for almost any other dance job you go on to do. I recollect a University ball at which we had to dance in a tent and get changed in a van parked around the back. The stage they had built specially for us meant that our heads touched the top of the tent. By the end of the show we looked like we'd had electric shocks from the static caused by the tent roof rubbing on our hair! You need to be versatile and be prepared to totally reshape your show for each place you visit. When touring around different venues you will be asked to do shows of different lengths and content. Sometimes the audience will consist of families, at other times it will be purely adult. You may be asked for a raunchy show or a family-oriented show with a special theme. Obviously you can't always create the perfect show, but it is a good idea to cover a broad spectrum of dance numbers when you start out. If all your routines are to Top 40 chart songs then a club having a French night won't be able to book you, but if you include a Can Can and a 70s routine or a number from a musical as well as raunchy and hip dance tracks, you will cover enough areas to be able to adapt your routines to suit all types of audience and venue.

If you are booked abroad you will normally be contracted for a limited number of shows in one or more venues. Some of the most rewarding contracts abroad can be when dance groups are flown out to war zones or to where the troops have been posted for months on end. You will be booked as part of a package show

Going on the road: 'X-Directory Dancers', Falklands

which means you are one element of the show along with a comedian, a singer, a magician or juggling fire eater. Dance groups are always booked as they don't have the budget to rehearse and choreograph a separate set of dancers, and the self-contained dance groups add a visual aspect to the show and boost the morale of lonely soldiers who are missing their families. You are invited to dine and chat with the officers after the shows, who pay you so much respect and treat you like royalty. After lugging your costumes around and driving yourself to gigs, you are suddenly being flown in helicopters and climbing in jeeps and being taken on an adventure miles from anywhere, often in the sunshine!

Resident dance groups

Some hotels, restaurants and clubs that host cabaret keep a resident dance group and band then invite other acts in to 'top the bill' for an evening. A resident show will usually have set shows for each night or a floorshow that is repeated during the evening. If you are resident in a holiday complex you may have to perform five or six different shows for each night of the week so the audience don't see the same thing every time. If other acts are in the show you will have more time to change and prepare for the next number. It is less hectic this way because you aren't the only attraction and it's not back-to-back dancing.

The advantage of a dancing contract like this is that you are still self-contained, but you stay in one place and have a company paying for everything. You will have a budget for certain costumes and for preparing specific numbers for the contract, for example Christmas or holiday numbers. You will be paid for rehearsal time, have dressing rooms to change in and your costumes will be looked after. Make sure that anything the company pays for, such as music and costumes, you can keep when you leave or buy back at a reduced price. You will also have a set time and place to dance, with proper distance between you and your audience (who will be sat down watching you, not standing over you as in some clubs).

Although touring is great fun, it is nice to have one place where you come to perform, and then leave knowing the time is yours and that you don't have to travel for miles to get home, sleep, then travel again the following day.

Chapter Eight

Music Industry

Most commercial dancers aspire to work in the music industry at some point during their career. This kind of dancing work is created by a band or pop group signing to a record label, and then embarking on a procedure of promotions to get the record played and the group seen in every possible place in order to break the band and get a smash hit. Dancers slot nicely into the promotions and are used almost everywhere to boost the image of pop music. Videos play an essential part in the profile of a single and are tailor-made for featuring dancers, and then there are the backing dancers needed for personal appearances in clubs, chat shows, children's TV, morning TV, *The National Lottery Show*, MTV, and so on. In fact these days a lot of the acts are the dancers! Joining a band or becoming a solo artiste is increasingly an option if you are an exceptional singer and dancer, and even fronting and miming are possible if you don't sing. The crucial element is your image. Having a 'look' is equally, if not more, important than having talent. Ideally you should have both, but many people succeed with just one strong quality – dancing, singing or image.

The music industry is largely based on who you know, and the best way in is to make contact with someone linked to a record company or pop group and work from there. A huge amount of business is done by word of mouth and as your career grows you will inevitably come across people involved in music. Some agencies have close ties with video production companies and artiste managements and supply all the dancers for particular record companies. Choreographers also build good relationships with the many industry people involved in launching new acts, and if success comes to the band they've choreographed they are likely to be asked to work on subsequent record releases. A Top 10 hit can therefore boost a choreographer's career! It is not quite the same for dancing and often different sets of dancers are used for different aspects of the record's promotion. For example, two of you may do a personal appearance (PA) tour while another two are booked to dance on all the television shows, and another two do the video shoot. This way more of you are employed, but if you're clever and learn how the industry operates (which will take time), it may be possible to land all these jobs and stick with the group for the forthcoming world tour!

The music industry is one of the biggest money-spinning industries in the world, and is full of wheeler dealers bartering over pop acts and trying to make money out of innocent wannabes. It's a complex business to understand and you must always seek independent legal advice before getting too involved. Friends of mine who have retired from this kind of dancing work feel as though they've learnt so much about the industry that their obvious next career move is to work for a record company or go into management.

Personal appearances

Personal Appearances or PAs are one way of promoting a record. The band or artiste performs (usually miming or singing along to a DAT tape) to audiences in clubs, or if it is more of a 'pop' record, at roadshows, shopping malls, and even schools. Dancers can perform as backing dancers or may even front the track, miming the lyrics and using dance as the main visual. This is how a lot of pop groups start out, playing for free just to be seen and heard and to judge the audience reaction to their music in a club environment. This is a great way to avoid spending huge budgets on showcase venues or splashing out on a video. Dancers on the other hand need to be provided with costumes and payment (the record company will normally foot the bill for this). Just because the band earns nothing doesn't mean you should. Dancing fees vary depending on the band's success; if they have had records released in the past and the record company have ploughed money into the whole project, you may find yourself on a decent wage for each performance and if you're lucky they will perform at two or three clubs each night. However, you may find yourself involved in a low budget project with an unknown band where your fees are low and you may even have to supply your own costumes.

A PA performance is usually choreographed and rehearsed a few days before you start touring. This means daytime rehearsals in the studio to put a show together. The record you will be promoting will only be about four minutes long and you may perform to another mix of the same track or one or two other tracks to make it worthwhile, but a club PA doesn't usually last longer than ten minutes which makes it possible to do a few in one night. Before Take That had a hit they performed in clubs for six months, sometimes doing five or six shows a night. This obviously took dedication but the hard work paid off in the end.

It is very tiring doing PAs as the clubs are spread out all over the country and you can cover hundreds of miles each night, but it can be beneficial too. If the band you're dancing for does well and has a hit record they will normally remain loyal to their dancers and keep them in the act for television performances and concert tours. From a dodgy club in Cleethorpes you could eventually find yourself dancing at Wembley!

PA work keeps you dancing and is great fun. The only disadvantages are the late nights, the amount of fast food you consume from motorway service stations, and the dodgy night-clubs you have to perform in (broken glass, spilt beer, pushy people). It's amazing the number of character-building moments you face. Your tour manager should deal with any problems and organise everything, and you will soon get to know the little team of people on the road – the band, the dancers, the tour manager, and the driver.

'Pop TV'

Many TV shows present music acts with backing dancers, and you may find yourself appearing on a different chat show every day of the week prior to a record release. Children's shows on a Saturday morning are favourites for young pop idols and great fun to dance on, but a bit of a squash by the time everyone is crammed on the set. If four dancers are booked to dance with a band on *Top Of The Pops*, then possibly only two will dance with the same band on children's TV. Space is always limited on these shows. The choreography for TV shows is likely to be the same as the choreography used in the video (if there was any). For most of the jobs you are collected from and returned to your home by chauffeured car, and you can turn up to the job in your dressing gown and slippers if you like – the make-up and wardrobe people will transform you from head to toe.

A booking such as *Top Of The Pops* is very rewarding because it is a prestigious show that you probably watched as a kid, and suddenly you find yourself there on the set! Many commercial dancers feel like they've accomplished their ambition once they've made it on to this show. An over-keen dancer, really a desperate groupie in disguise, who knocks on the door of Robbie Williams' manager's office, will do herself no favours. You need to work hard to get your foot in the door of this kind of work

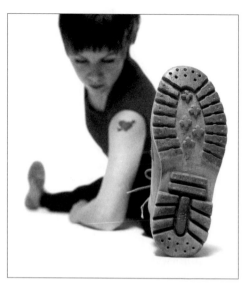

PHOTO: HILARY SHEDEL/ARENA IMAGES

and if you are successful enough to get an audition you have to prove your worth as a dancer and, equally importantly, with your image. The music industry is full of people with a great look or vibe.

There are many perks to this kind of job, the greatest being to meet or dance with your pop idols and 'hang out' with them backstage, not to mention the limousine rides and aftershow party invites!

Videos

Dancers shoot videos for acts that don't even make the Top 100 in the UK chart! Videos came into vogue in the early 80s and since then have become the backbone of a record's promotion. Fans love to have an image to go alongside their favourite tracks, and fortunately dancers are a regular ingredient in the making of music videos. Music television shows the broad selection of dancers and dance styles used in videos. American acts in particular portray the excellent skill of the dancers in their videos. British videos tend to be incredibly creative, but are often too fast to be able to absorb the dancing talents.

Video shoots mean long days. Directors often try to create special effects and use obscure lighting patterns, and you may find yourself dancing in a cold warehouse with nothing but a tea urn to keep you company. A favourite technique is dancing in front of a blue backdrop, when the background is added later by computer (bluescreening), or being hoisted up on a safety wire to simulate flying. This is all fun but tiring. After the eleventh take of a dance routine in dry ice on a concrete floor, your patience and professionalism is tested, especially when only three seconds will be seen in the final cut. Costumes are another wonder of video shoots – 60s, 70s, and 80s looks, spacesuits, catsuits and swimsuits – you could be asked to wear anything! Video storyboards can vary from the ordinary to the extreme, so be warned.

Payment for video shoots varies and depends on the production company involved. Some shoots are low budget and last minute. The director may book ten dancers he knows, pay you cash in hand for a ten-hour day and tell you to bring along all your friends to be extras in return for free food and drink! Other shoots take weeks of preparation and the video company appoints a casting director to hold a casting for featured dancers. This work usually comes via your agent and is organised properly. Video shoots are notorious for going overtime and if you are released after 12 hours you've done well. Your agent will negotiate an overtime rate should you exceed the standard ten-hour day (very likely) and ensure you get enough breaks. Video work can be fun to work on, however. You are dancing, you are working with friends, and you are probably dressed up and performing a completely 'off the wall' routine.

Being in a band

More and more dancers are wising up to the fact that joining a band is a way in to the recording industry, and with girl and boy bands currently being so popular, record companies are scouting stage schools for new talent. Members of the Spice Girls trained at dance colleges and artistes such as Billie were plucked from theatre school. It is certainly an avenue that dancers with a certain level of singing ability should explore. After all, why be on

Top Of The Pops dancing *behind* them when you could *be* them. It is easier said than done, however, and for every 50 girl/boy bands, only one makes it. Few make a lot of money from it – usually the songwriters or the groups with huge fan bases and merchandise sales – as record companies are far too big and clever to make it an easy career and managers are often sly and greedy. If you reach the stage at which you need a manager, make sure you trust them; don't get swept away by a manager who promises you the limousine lifestyle.

If you are genuinely interested in recording and your singing voice is exceptional, then you could start by hooking up with a songwriter or producer to get some material together, or find a way of getting your voice recorded to tape while covering a song. There are all kinds of karaoke machines and backing tapes available. Don't waste time sending copies to recording companies; they won't be listened to and it won't reach the right person. It would be better to wait until you find a contact in the industry via your dancing work. Your dance agents will often get approached by record companies or promoters and they can vet them first before sending you along to meet them. Ask their advice. The best way to break into the recording industry is through the creative side rather than the management side, and anyway you won't need managing for a while. Be your own boss in the beginning. Put up notices in reputable recording and rehearsal studios advertising your services as a backing vocalist or session singer (you can use your agent's phone number if you prefer not to give out your own). You might even find a band that needs a singer. But don't jump in feet first and fall for adverts from people offering you immediate stardom. Think carefully and never sign any agreements without first seeking independent legal advice.

If you seriously want to be *in* a band, not just backing for them or fronting tracks, but actually signed to a record label, it is worth remembering that you will not be allowed to do other dancing work, as you will be 'exclusively' signed to the label. To make a decent living you will have to be very successful, so don't throw away your dancing career with high expectations of becoming a pop star. For further advice I suggest you consult *All You Need To Know About The Music Business* by Donald Passman (Simon & Schuster).

Fronting

If you'd like to enter the recording industry but your singing voice isn't strong enough to actually record, then consider fronting. Dancers are perfect for fronting tracks as it is all about image and great dancing as the focal point of the band. You don't need to worry about the vocals, just produce some convincing miming! The majority of tracks that need fronting are dance tracks that make their way into the clubs and become hit records without a band attached to them. They are normally mixed by DJs who have no visual act to perform PAs or appear on TV shows to sell more records, so they turn to funky looking dancers who can give the act an image. You will perform to a DAT and receive a one-off fee for the gig. There is little chance of becoming signed to a recording company as an artiste if you are just fronting an act, and it is safer to receive a fee each time you perform. If you get involved with contracts and royalties you will not get paid for months, and as a lot of these records are short-lived, whether they are hits or not, they need to sell huge amounts for a single to actually make you any money. Having said that, if you become the focal point for the act for more than one record release you may find yourself in a stronger position to negotiate a contract with the record company or increase your fees. If the act has become well-known with your face attached to it, they often have no choice in the matter (this is where a manager may come in handy to negotiate for you).

Some girl/boy bands also require fronters. Maybe two or three members of the group can sing well, but they need two or three others who just look great or dance well. You may not earn as much as the singing members, but can still have great rewards if the group are successful.

Making it big!

Being in a successful band or dancing for a well-known artiste introduces a whole new set of rules. Suddenly you are performing on a bigger scale, your club PA tour has become a sell-out world concert tour, the video you featured in has been nominated for an award, and the records you are dancing to have gone platinum in nine countries!

World tours create a huge buzz and the auditions are often impressive publicity stunts and an ordeal for dancers. They are sometimes kept top secret, as deciphering dancers from groupies is not an easy job. Agents may step in and make the auditions private affairs, inviting only top quality dancers from their books so only the most outstanding dancers walk away with the work. Music awards are also massive industry events and seen as a prestigious job for a dancer to be involved in. *The Brits*, *The MTV Awards* and *The* Smash Hits *Poll Winners Party*, are all huge televised live shows. To dance at an event of this kind is an achievement for a commercial dancer. These jobs normally come about when a band you've danced for have been nominated for an award or asked to perform live on the show, and you are booked to backing dance for them.

Everybody has an idea of the fame that comes with being a pop star and it is appealing to most types of performers, but the work involved and the chances of being successful are slim and commercial dancers should be aware of the pitfalls. You have to learn to cope with the fans, the crowds, the interviews and the invasion of your private life. 'Yes,' I hear you say, 'that's exactly what I want!' I'm sure it is, and why not? The level of dancing and size of the shows you'll be involved in is more than a dancer could ask for, but it is worth remembering that you have behind the scenes secrets that the paparazzi would love to get hold of. As a professional dancer in the public eye you have a responsibility to keep your head together and set an example. The dancer who gets horrifically drunk or dishes dirt to reporters on the artiste they work for, will not do. Backing dancing and fronting are great alternatives to this lifestyle. You get to travel with the band, have time off while others are writing and recording albums, and you retain your privacy, while still enjoying the luxuries of travelling first class or eating in nice places without the added worry of contracts, lawyers or record sales. You get a fee for your day's work and the bigger the act becomes, the bigger your fee gets. Enjoy the success and gather the rewards, but tread carefully. Good luck!

Chapter Nine

Modelling

The model dancer

Modelling is a complete vocation in itself, but some dancers manage to combine their dancing career with some sort of modelling. If you have been gifted with the necessary vital statistics and you are at least 5ft 8in tall you may be able to get into modelling. Models require good teeth, clear skin, healthy hair, good hands and nails and regular features. Like a dancer, a model must be reliable and very professional. It is a competitive industry and tough to become established; very few reach 'supermodel' status. A lot of commercial dancing jobs naturally involve modelling, such as dancing shows that present fashion clothes or advertise sportsgear. These are known as trade shows.

If you are not gifted in the height stakes, but are very pretty with a shapely figure, you may consider glamour modelling or get involved with a glamour girl or guy roadshow (this may involve basic dancing). The idea behind this type of work is to be sexy but beware – you may have to wear skimpy underwear or go topless.

Photographic work covers a wide spectrum of work and is not just a job for the stunning. If you do have 'the look of the decade', however, you could find yourself on the cover of a glossy magazine. This is known as editorial modelling and is the most prestigious type of photographic work. For the rest of us, photographers often require dancers' physiques for shoots, even if it has nothing to do with dancing. Dancers are toned and have a knack of contorting their bodies into funny positions and this is useful to a photographer trying to shoot a leg suspended in mid-air for a hosiery product! Once you have made a few contacts and begun working as a commercial dancer you may find that some kind of modelling work follows on. Your agent will certainly be called for photographic castings, and you may also get involved in promotional work. Promotional agencies use dancers and models for advertising campaigns and company promotions. This

Modelling

PHOTO: SERGIO BONDIONI

type of work has no height restrictions, but needs well-presented people with outgoing personalities.

Trade/fashion shows

Trade shows are corporate events and involve staging a show using a combination of modelling and dancing to promote a product. They can be produced specifically for an in-house company conference, a worldwide industry trade fair or they can be used at large exhibitions open to the public. Sometimes fashion companies link up with sponsors and put on shows using dancers, for example Peugeot cars may sponsor Dorothy Perkins and present a fashion show at The Motor Show to attract attention to the cars they are exhibiting. Ten dancers dancing on the bonnet of a Ford Escort does wonders for audience attention!

Dancers are often used to promote a product to do with action, for example to sell sportswear. The latest skiwear range looks far better in a dynamic show full of dancers representing the sport in the form of a dance, rather than modelled on a straightforward catwalk. The choreography may well simulate the sport, so don't be surprised to find yourself dancing in a boxing ring wearing baggy satin shorts and impersonating Prince Naseem! Trade shows are immense fun for dancers – there is something terribly satisfying about strutting to loud funky music then suddenly breaking into a dance routine. This kind of work usually comes from an agency, and very occasionally an advert for a trade show will appear, but the contracts are always linked to choreographers who have found the work and production companies who put on the full show.

Fashion shows use models on a catwalk, an elongated stage that juts out into the audience. Catwalk shows are designed to show off fashion and it is usually left to the 6ft models to specialise in this type of modelling. However, these shows are increasingly produced by choreographers and if you are a tall dancer he may bear you in mind for his shows, but remember that you are not wearing specially designed costumes with American tan tights securely in place. You may be showing lingerie and feel half naked or you could feel like you're about to pass out under a huge wedding dress. Dancing as such is not required for this kind of show (unless the choreographer feels inclined to incorporate it). You are a moving clothes horse. You must be able to catwalk – it's amazing how many dancers cannot strut coolly in time to the music, holding their head up and keeping good deportment. Dancers often try too hard when 'walking' and look, ironically, uncoordinated. You need to be able to casually twirl, not technically turn, and be able to slip jackets on and off without hesitating over buttons. The final, and one of the most crucial requirements of a fashion show is what dancers are good at – quick changes!

Dancers are also regularly used in hair shows because they are required to do more than just walk. A designer with an adventurous idea may ask the choreographer to create weird and wonderful shapes for his dancers, whilst carrying a hair style of tree branches steadily down a catwalk. They use the same format as a fashion show, but the fashion is hair rather than clothes.

For all fashion, hair and trade shows, whether you are dancer or model or both, height and figure are of the essence and to be considered you need to be 5ft 8in tall (preferably more) and the perfect clothes peg. Sportswear shows may also require high muscle definition to accentuate lycra wear. The nice thing about a contract of this kind is that you are usually booked for at least a week and get to work in a team environment without it dragging on or becoming like a regular job. In a short period of time the dancers, models and choreographer all pull together and create a great buzz before the performances. The pressure is on to rehearse quickly and properly, and there are many teething problems as clothing is the main subject of the show, so dancers are constantly pulled out of rehearsals for fittings. This means that rehearsals are difficult and disjointed, and makes for a very frustrated choreographer. Fees for trade or fashion shows can be good; you will receive rehearsal pay and per diems or be fed and watered. If the contract is out of town your hotel accommodation will be paid for, and the fees for the actual shows are generally above average, and very good if it is a well-known industry. As ever, it varies depending on the client and the size and number of shows. Some exhibitions, for example, put on three or four shows per day for seven to ten days – hard work, but excellent pay.

Glamour

Glamour modelling is another option for dancers, although not one that is often followed up. Glamour work can be extremely successful for someone who can dance well, but it is not for the easily offended. It can involve photographic or live work. The most obvious examples are 'Page 3' and calendar modelling, but there are many other kinds of glamour modelling jobs. To get into this line of work, however, you need to be willing to take off your clothes.

Glamour work would suit a dancer with a fuller figure and a bust size of not less than 36in. You are able to get away with being as small as 5ft 2in but once again looks and figure are important. As the title suggests, the type of model needed is very *glamorous*, hence dancers are often perfect, with their sun-tanned bodies, bleached, bright or big hair, sassy clothing and often large personalities! Glamour models may be booked for their boobs, bum or pecs, but they can also be used for photographic work which does not necessarily require nudity or insinuate sex. Jobs include shower or water advertisements, health and medical literature, swimwear or underwear catalogues, sex guide books, and the newspaper and magazine shoots that advertise absolutely anything using a voluptuous, good-looking, sexy model (male or female!) beside the product: beer, tyres, peanuts, double glazing . . .

Glamour work is well paid, but can be hard to handle. It is always best to work through a glamour model agency, rather than directly, so the client or photographer are vetted first and you do not get involved in something you regret. Small newspaper adverts with clever wording are the most suspicious. Don't send off photographs (especially nude or semi-nude) to adverts or addresses you know nothing about. Try and do some research first and don't give out contact addresses or phone numbers until you are 100 per cent sure of the recipient. Pornography is very different to glamour.

There are many dancers, male and female, who earn good money doing glamour shows on the night-club circuit. They have all kinds of names, the most famous being The Ann Summers Roadshow and The Chippendales. Their floorshows are done wearing very skimpy costumes and are very raunchy. They can appear tacky and under-rehearsed, but are entertaining for the broadminded. The dance moves are basic and mainly involve parading around dressed up as a policewoman or Tarzan. These glamour roadshows are designed to be sexy and appeal to the opposite sex, and are very popular on hen and stag nights. Showing off stunning bodies is the object of the game, and the shows often involve stripping on stage or getting a member of the audience to do it for them. It is sometimes possible to get a job as a dressed dancer to do a raunchy solo in the middle of the show, giving a taste of quality dancing while the others do a quick change. A good living can be made doing these kind of shows providing you don't mind travelling up and down the motorway, you are over 18, and you are not shy of the full monty!

Photographic work

Photographic work is not only for supermodels or geared towards high-profile editorials (glossy magazines). Think about the things you see every day – advertisements featuring 'normal' looking people, leaflets for double glazing showing a workman rather than a Calvin Klein model, brochures for shopping centres or restaurants showing a middle-aged couple rather than Caprice. Think about the things you see which would suit photogenic dancers – book covers, album sleeves, shower ads, fitness and health brochures, magazine articles connected to dance, and so on. A photographic model does not have height restrictions but must have at least one striking feature, whether it be amazing hair or perfect fingernails, as they may be booked to photograph that particular part of their body. Photographic work is not necessarily associated with just 'good looks'; there is an agency in London with a reputation for booking 'uglies', people with character or a quirky looking face.

Photographic work is perfect for dancers to pursue if they can find it. There is work for all ages and all looks, but it is inconsistent unless you are a full-time model working away at your career, going to see photographers and attending two or three castings a day. Many dancing jobs involve photographers and are the perfect opportunity to introduce yourself to them on an informal basis. For example, if you were booked on a pop promotional video, a photographer will usually arrive on the day to take some stills. If you can chat to him during the job he will get to know your face, and if you are lucky he may ask you if you model as well as dance, but either way you may someday bump into him again when he is holding a casting. If you are a familiar face it will help, especially if he knows you have been successfully booked on dancing jobs before. It is essential to make contacts and to sell yourself.

If you are serious about your work you must endeavour to look your best at all times. This is difficult for dancers who work odd hours and spend a lot of time 'on the road' or in sweaty rehearsal rooms, but if you intend modelling you need to have plenty of rest and a healthy lifestyle (see 'looking after yourself'). The competition is tough and of 40 blonde girls at a casting for a photographic shoot, the one with healthy skin and teeth will walk away with the work, *not* the one with bags under her eyes. When you are booked for a photographic job it is worth asking if a make-up artist is supplied, as turning up to a shoot fully made-up will result in the make-up artist having to take it all off and start again, leaving you feeling rather worn and tight-skinned. Don't arrive to a job ready made-up unless asked to do so. Just use a good moisturiser, dab on a bit of spot cover-up or lip balm and leave the rest to them. Even if you do have to do your own make-up, do it at the studio under the correct lighting and after a discussion with the photographer.

Photographic work can be extremely well paid, especially if it is for an advertising campaign. You are normally paid by the hour with a minimum booking of two hours. This is great if you are only used for half an hour, but most unusual as the make-up artist will take that long to get you ready. The advantage comes when you receive more money for 'usage'. This means the client would like to sell your picture on to promote a product further, use it around the world, or perhaps let it appear in the same magazine for five years. If this is the case you will be offered extra fees in the form of a royalty or a 'buy-out', a lump sum that gives them full rights to the photo, entitling them to use it when and where they like. Your agent will negotiate the best deal for you. The majority of photographic shoots are very straightforward and command a fee similar to a day's dancing work. The photographer keeps the copyright of the picture, and you give your consent to appear in the shot at the time of the initial booking. For more information on this kind of work contact the Association of Model Agents.

A photographic session

PHOTO: SERGIO BONDIONI

Promotional work

Promotional work can include anything from handing out leaflets at Waterloo Station to sitting in a Jeep at the Motor Show. If a company is launching a new product or pushing for more business they will promote in the most ingenious ways at exhibitions, parties, sporting events, supermarkets, pubs, theme parks and festivals, using a promotional team to add colour and glamour and attract attention. Sometimes promotional models and dancers are asked to wear clothing with a brand name on and do nothing except socialise and look good, while a stand at the Ideal Home Exhibition promoting foot spas is far more appealing if a model in a red swimsuit demonstrates how to use it, rather than a business man with his trouser legs rolled up. You occasionally get contracts that combine promotional and dancing work such as the Marlborough Roadshow. The organisers pick a team of models/dancers to help launch an advertising campaign at the major motor racing events and in nightclubs around the country, and the Roadshow usually involves a choreographed show, a photo session, handouts of promotional samples and leaflets, and competitions.

Promotional work is not just about looking pretty and it's not just work for girls. Promotional teams need male and female, intelligent, confident people who feel easy talking to the general public. You may be miked up and put on a rostrum to talk to an audience about a product, and may need to study products like mobile phones, toys or computers before the promotion, to find out exactly how they work. If this is necessary you will be invited to a training day prior to the engagement (you usually receive expenses or a fee for this). You are not expected to be a salesperson or a supervisor unless you are specifically booked and trained for the job; additional staff from the company will be on site to do this. You are a promotional person employed to enhance the product by looking a certain way, or by doing or saying something specific. One of the easiest but most tedious jobs is leafleting. Standing in a cold train station at 7a.m., trying to alert grumpy commuters with an A5 leaflet on roof tiles can be pretty dull. The most fun jobs are those for which you have to dress up as the product – a giant walking ice-cream certainly turns heads!

Chapter Ten

Alternative Work

Club dancing

Club dancing sounds suspicious and most people jump to conclusions when you tell them you dance in a club, but in fact there is a wide spectrum of dance jobs within the club circuit, and many different clubs – country clubs, hostess clubs, night-clubs and more recently table dancing clubs. Each type of club houses a different type of dancer and they don't all involve taking your clothes off. On the contrary, only the table dancers undress.

Club dancing is an excellent way of keeping fit and earning money while still having plenty of time for auditions and jobs. Because the work is at night you can build your dancing career during the day *and* pay your bills. However you do need a fair amount of stamina to work around the clock and you must be careful to pace yourself. You also need to be very wary of working late and make sure that you can get home safely; travel with a friend or take the car if you have one. You will receive a lot of attention working in a club. You dance very near the audience and need to be aware of the public becoming too friendly either before you dance, afterwards or even during.

Podium dancing

Podium dancing is exactly as the name suggests – you dance on a podium, platform, or in a cage. Night-clubs and sometimes fun pubs employ podium dancers to dance freestyle to the music being played by the DJ. It is a glorified version of disco dancing but on a much bigger scale. You are a pacemaker for the crowd, there to provide inspiration and get everybody dancing and enjoying themselves. You need to be an extrovert dancer and not mind improvising on the spot. You have no idea what records will be played and you must adapt your style each time. A good way of making sure you don't dry up is to practise some of your ideas at

Podium dancer   PHOTO: RODNEY FORT

home in front of the mirror and rehearse little medleys which can fit to almost anything.

Some clubs play hardcore music all night which can be exhausting and tedious as some dance remixes repeat themselves for 12 minutes. Other clubs dedicate whole sections of the evening to one era, and you have to dance 20 minutes of 60s music, then 20 minutes of 70s and so on. If you are old enough to remember all the old styles of dance then this is an easy life. One night's podium dancing will be approximately four hours long, but you are not expected to dance for all that time. You will be asked to dance in 20–30-minute slots and then take a break for the same length of time, so you end up dancing approximately two hours a night. This is an excellent workout and keeps you fit. You will be expected to provide your own costumes, which don't have to be professionally made but should stand out from the crowd. It is an ideal opportunity to dress up in things you would normally feel silly wearing. Theme outfits are always popular, for example, dressing up like a cowboy or wearing a policeman's outfit, or you could try basing yourself on a pop star like Madonna or Puff Daddy. Payment for podium dancers varies and is not as much as you would receive for a day's professional dancing job, but if you can podium for three or four nights a week you will end up with a fair wage for a week's work. Podium dancing is the perfect job to boost your income and help you keep fit without interrupting your dancing career.

Table dancing

Dancing is a form of entertainment and a skilled occupation. Dancers train very hard and eventually they start work professionally in a particular field of the dancing industry. Table dancing is not strictly speaking a 'form' of dance, and you don't need to train for it. It is not 'commercial dance' but it does go on in clubs and is becoming increasingly popular, so I feel it should be covered in this book.

The object of table dancing is to dance freestyle at a table or on a platform, with the audience sat around you and watching you as you move. You are expected to slowly undress to the music, taking layers of clothing off while you dance, but keeping your shoes on (high heels only, no trainers or jazz shoes I'm afraid). Members of the audience are only allowed to touch you to give you money, by sliding it into your shoe (if that's all you have on) or handing it to you. Table dancing is performed by females only (at the moment) and it is of a particular style, specifically designed for the opposite sex to enjoy. Table dancing clubs are stylish as opposed to seedy and the lighting is very dim. There may be long metal poles from floor to ceiling for the dancers to twist around. Table dancers need an excellent figure, smooth skin, and beautiful make-up and hair. Your body is what the audience want to see, and the most important element is that you must be open-minded and prepared to dance naked.

As you would imagine, the fees for taking off your clothes are excellent, but it is a tips-only wage. The club owners do not pay you, in fact you have to pay them to dance in their club! They will decide whether or not you are right for table dancing and they may pay for you to have a course of sunbeds or a make-over. Some clubs have facilities on-site for beautifying yourself, because it is such an important factor of the job. Once you have been groomed you can start work. Depending on the size of the club the dancers work to a rota. About 20 girls a night will work, with 5–20 dancing at any one time depending on the number of customers. You can earn a week's wages in one night if you're busy; from your total earnings you must give a percentage to the club, the rest is yours. Table dancing clubs are huge in America, and the standard of dancing is high. A flexible trained dancer will be very successful, but you have to be sure it's what you want to do – is it what you set your heart on when you decided to become a professional dancer? You can be easily swayed because the money is very good, and if you haven't worked for two months it can be tempting. Make sure you know what's involved and talk to the other dancers in the club before you jump in feet first. The dancing is not choreographed and your audience is not there to appreciate your dance ability so think about your career before you get used to the money. There is nothing wrong with table dancing – it is not prostitution, but neither is it like any other form of dance which requires the skills you already have and could use.

Cheerleading

Cheerleading is becoming increasingly popular in the UK, while in the US it is almost part of a commercial dancer's training! It stems from American high schools and a lot of dancers got started that way – choreographer and dancer Paula Abdul began her career as a cheerleader. Cheerleading is used mainly for team sports such as basketball, American football and on the odd occasion for rugby and soccer. It is designed to cheer on your team and encourage their fans to gee them up into winning! Throughout the game you break into chants and do small routines, and if your team scores it is your job to jump up and down and yell like mad!

Cheerleading is not only performed by dancers, as fitness and aerobics instructors are also used regularly. The dancing is very aerobic in style and has boxy patterns suitable for pitch sidelines and for keeping straight lines. The arm movements are quite regimented, especially if pom poms are used and the routines are full of round-offs or dancing in cannon (i.e. one after another). It is quite mechanical, and fascinating to watch when danced well. Often you will be asked to do a pre-match routine in the centre of the court or field. For this you will perform a longer, more involved routine and dance to a track to get the audience going. The cheerleading team will have a huge repertoire of very short routines, all to different tracks which they will rotate throughout a game. Being a cheerleader is very much like being part of a sporting team. If you happen to work for an American coach you will most definitely do exercises in rehearsal time to bring you together like a team. For them it is not just about the moves, it is to be 'in touch' with each other and know your team members so well that you become a unit and reflect that in the performance. I recall the majority of my rehearsal time as a cheerleader sat in a circle with our choreographer and the cheerleading team playing 'getting to know you' games and 'finding ourselves'. It was a bit of a shock at first, but some of her philosophies really did help our dancing and team spirit.

Cheerleading has several perks. If you work for a successful team or sport you could find yourself travelling to support your team wherever they go (all expenses paid, of course). If they have a big sponsor you could find yourself bombarded with freebies and sports gear, and if your team becomes famous you could find yourself in their shadow, undertaking hundreds of promotional jobs in their absence and receiving a nice fee for turning up to open a supermarket and having your photo taken with three of your cheerleading team mates. Unfortunately you can also be labelled as dumb and treated like a 'bimbo' for being a cheer-leader, but some dancers don't mind this. All those I've known have stood their ground and made a point of not playing up to this role. It is still thought of as a job for sexy girls in short skirts, but it is a lot more funky now and some teams have introduced male dancers. You will be contracted for a minimum number of games, but if your team is knocked out of a tournament you could find yourself without as much work as you'd planned. Seasons are short for most of the cheerleading sports, but they are fun con-tracts to have while they last.

Temping

It is worth remembering that if you decide to take the path of a seasonal dancer there will undoubtedly be 'in-between times', periods when you have finished one job but have six weeks or more until you begin a new contract. This is not necessarily a bad thing, but something a dancer should be very aware of. A sensible idea would be to save some of your wages to last you over this period, then you can feel safe knowing that even if nothing else turns up you can still get by financially.

You may not want to take on other work, but enjoy the time away from dancing and catch up on other things in 'the real world', or you may be able to find short contracts to fit in-between your seasons. Maybe the acts you have worked with before will ask you to do some gigs with them, or there may be opportunities to dep (stand in) for fellow dancers, for example, if they want time off from a regular dancing job like a residency, you could be the perfect substitute to fill a short gap in their contract. As well as jobs like podium dancing in clubs, there is film and TV extra work which are perfect for paying the rent. Extra work can be dull; the hours are long and the days start early, but you are fed three good meals a day and if you take along a good book it's pretty easy money, especially when you run into overtime. Promotional work is also a temporary alternative, and it is worth joining a promotional agency specifically for this kind of work – you don't need to be available for work all the time, you can just check in with them when you want to.

Aside from actual dancing work, you may have teaching qualifications, and a lot of dancers find their way back to their original dancing school to earn extra pennies. If you are lucky enough to have any word processing/computer or secretarial skills, you could also sign to an agency who will find you temporary positions doing administrative, reception or telesales work. You should be aware that temp work is an alternative and not the end of the world. These suggestions are to help your annual income, they are not major career moves.

Chapter Eleven

Special Skills

Special skills include anything you are competent at doing in addition to dancing. When I say *anything*, I am referring to a physical skill (although being computer literate and having 120 wpm listed on your CV may come in handy one day). If you have any hidden talents it is certainly worth mentioning it to your agent or printing it on your CV. The stilt-walking course you did last summer may land you the biggest TV commercial of your career; the more obscure the skill the less competition there will be. This doesn't mean you should rush out and book up a series of balloon-flying lessons. It is just worth being aware of any techniques you have picked up on your travels, even if it is a popular one like juggling. If you have the look and the skill then you're in with a chance of work especially on TV commercials – the advertising companies regularly ask for special skills and sports for their product launch ideas.

Special skills for dancing jobs are likely to be tricks that are very visual on stage, for example:

- acrobatics
- gymnastics
- aerobics
- robotics
- break dancing
- body-popping
- baton twirling
- moon walking
- roller skating/blading
- skate boarding
- stunt artiste
- pointe work
- trampolinist
- trapeze
- flamenco
- limbo

- jiving
- Latin American
- line dancing.

A choreographer could incorporate these skills into a stage show to enhance the dancing, add depth to a performance or break up a continuous dancing show. Acrobatics and street dancing skills such 'breaking and locking' are the most popular and are regularly seen in videos and trade shows, but like everything it goes in trends. In the 80s circus skills were popular, and everyone was swinging on high wires and jumping from chandeliers in their videos. Don't worry if you don't have any special skills; you don't *need* them, you are a dancer not a circus clown so stay focused on your dancing and the type of work that suits you. Different people with different abilities, sizes and looks will suit different jobs as you will find out.

That little extra something!

It is a great feeling when you 'shine' at an audition, and if you can provide that little extra something the client is looking for, then the job will be yours. This often comes in the form of a special skill, a striking look or simply the right ingredients on the right day. You may be the only dancer in the room with her pointe shoes in her bag. If you go to an open audition and the choreographer asks if anybody has any special skills and you can muster up 20 fouettes on pointe, they will be impressed and remember your face, even if it's not the extra something they were thinking of. Be warned, however, stepping forward to do a half-hearted cartwheel into a forward roll will not be greatly appreciated, especially when everyone gathers round to see what you are about to perform. At least make sure you can manage a neat walkover into splits before passing yourself off as an acrobat. It's great to push yourself to try and stand out from the rest, and knowing you have more strings to your bow will give you more confidence and may get you the job – it's a bit like playing your 'ace card'. But if you can't present it well enough don't attempt to try as you may do more harm than good by wasting time.

If you are considering listing half a dozen sporting skills that you haven't done since school on your CV, then be careful – limit

Special skills

PHOTO: HILARY SHEDEL/ARENA IMAGES

them to just one or two and make sure you have time to brush up
on them in time for an audition. It is pointless listing countless
dodgy skills as you will end up in a panic if you are asked to perform them on spec. Include no more than four exceptional skills
on your CV and make sure two of them are of a high standard and
two are at least passable. After all, the chances of you having to do
them on a dancing job are pretty remote, but nevertheless
possible!

Chapter Twelve

Been There, Seen it, Done it!

You've seen the movies, you've watched *Top Of The Pops*, you've been to ballet, tap and modern dance classes since you were a child, and you've perfected your drag-runs across the kitchen floor, but there is nothing quite like hearing it from the horse's mouth!

Dee Dee Wilde of Pan's People – the famous dancers of the 1970s – was most well-known for her weekly appearances on BBC's *Top Of The Pops* and from there moved on to many other TV variety shows. Younger dancers may be familiar with her dance studios in London 'The Dance Attic'. Dee Dee has covered tremendous ground in the dancing industry and her dedication has set a fine example to many dancers.

I also linked up with some working dancers to find out exactly how their dancing careers started, which direction they went in and where they are now . . .

Dee Dee Wilde

Where did you train?
Elmhurst Ballet School in Camberley, Surrey.

When did you start dancing?
Before I was born my mother was told by a fortune-teller that I was going to be in the theatre. So as a baby I always walked on my toes and desperately wanted to be a ballerina. I pestered my mother until she gave in, and finally at the age of three I attended my first ballet class. When I was almost ten I auditioned for Elmhurst and spent the next seven years boarding there while my parents lived in Africa. I only saw them once a year in the summer, which was very hard to cope with. But it didn't deter me from my ambition to become a dancer.

Any dancer will tell you, you have to train incredibly hard to achieve excellence. If you're a dancer you have to train every day

Dee Dee Wilde   ASSOCIATED PRESS/REX FEATURES

to keep your body fit and supple; it's hard if you're tired, but you have to keep the discipline up, so it's very much a dedicated profession.

You were a member of the famous dancing group, Pan's People. When did it start and how did you become so well-known?

Originally we were in a group called 'The Beat Girls' and we were rehearsing in Earl's Court. The gentleman who owned the building said there was an audition to dance on *Top Of The Pops*, which every dancer always wants to appear on. It was the next day and for a choreographer called Virginia Mason. We all went along to the audition and Ruth and I got the job. So the very first time I ever appeared on TOTP was with another group, dancing to an inspiring little number called 'Simple Simon Says'. While we were doing a camera rehearsal Ruth spotted an old friend, a director from the BBC. After the show we took him off to the bar and chatted him up and said, 'If you ever need a new group to dance on the show instead of Virginia's, well . . .', and he was true to his word – it was only a few weeks later in March 1968 that we got our break and were asked to appear regularly on *Top Of The Pops*. Firstly, our appearances were once a month, then after a year we were contracted for 13-week periods, renewable, which meant we appeared every week of the year! We were very much in the public eye, for in those days TOTP was one of the most highly-viewed programmes in the whole of British television; 17 million people tuned in each week.

A typical week went like this: three days doing *Top Of The Pops*, then guest-starring on other variety shows, like Frankie Howerd, Bobbie Gentry or John Denver. Once a month we would fly off to Belgium and Holland to host and dance in shows, then we'd tear back to do the personal appearances which were coming in thick and fast. With the TV exposure our fame was spreading. We were getting busier and busier. The public were always amazed at how much rehearsing we did and they never realised a dancer's life could be so arduous.

The peak of Pan's People's fame was 1972–74 in the days when myself, Babs, Louise Clarke, Ruth Pearson and Cherry Gillespie were together (Cherry took over from Andrea Rutherford, the other blonde bombshell, who got married, had a child and left). We knew we had arrived while guesting on a show with Jimmy Saville, when Mary Whitehouse was outraged by our costumes. Our dresses with low-cut fronts and slits right up to our arses were just too much for her! She complained bitterly to the media and we became infamous.

The choreography of Pan's People was a real inspiration. Where did it come from?
Flick Colby was our choreographer. She hailed from America where she was a member of The Joffery Ballet Company. When she left and came to England at about 20 years old she joined us and took over as choreographer. She brought new and innovative steps with her, which were very individual and rather quirky, mixed with a touch of sensuality which seemed to work. It was all very raunchy. Flick was very aware of her own sexuality and ours as women, and this always came across.

In the 70s Pan's People were the supermodels of their time. Do you think history could repeat itself with a new group of dancers?
To achieve the sort of fame the Spice Girls have for instance would be very difficult without another string to one's bow like singing. It sounds terribly clichéd, but there is not as much opportunity these days as when I was a dancer. There's a far better choice of training, but there are not enough jobs to go round, especially television jobs. Contradicting myself, I do think that if a group was formed who were excellent dancers, based on the idea of Pan's People, with the right people behind them, yes I think

they could do well. After all, at the end of the day it's all to do with talent and management.

How did Pan's People come to an end?
Slowly, very gradually. The first one to go was Louise Clarke. She met her future husband and left the group to be with him and then, blow of blows to every man in England, Babs fell in love with Robert Powell. He had just been offered the role of 'Jesus Christ' and was off to film in Morocco for nine months. Babs obviously wanted to be with him, so they got married right away and that was Babs gone. From the original group this left myself, Ruth and Cherry, but in December of the same year I quit too. So then most of the group had gone. Even though the dancers who replaced us were very competent, we were known individually and had built up quite a following so Pan's People only continued for about six months and ended in 1976.

Do you realise you were role models for a whole generation of dancers?
I don't think we realised we were role models until we started becoming incredibly popular and getting fan mail. To begin with it was just a very exciting thing to be able to do, we were very young. To be dancing, which was one's vocation, earning money and being successful, then on top of that having fame too, was a wonderful situation. We did realise that we were becoming role models so as ambassadors of dance we were very careful of our image and reputation.

Who do you think dancers look up to nowadays?
Well this is the extraordinary thing. In my day our icons were Margot Fonteyn and Nureyev. These days kids are influenced not by dancers, but by the pop world. I'd say 95 per cent of kids who like dancing watch *Top Of The Pops* and say 'I want to be like that'. For classical or more technical dance, I would say Darcey Bussell, Sylvie Guilem and still Wayne Sleep are the strongest influences, and judging by the hundreds of girls who turned up at the auditions at my studio, Michael Flatley seems to wield a lot of power. *River Dance* put Irish dancing on the map.

Do you think dancing should return to TV shows?
I do, but the trouble is the format of those kinds of show is very

old hat, and in this day and age variety shows look terribly dated. The nearest thing now is *The National Lottery*, *The Des O'Connor Show* and *Stars In Their Eyes*, which is excellent and has a clever idea behind it. I do actually think it would be great to go right back to dance films like the ones Fred and Ginger did with huge Hollywood numbers. One could make them more modern and put them back on the screen. I think there is a market for that but it's probably far too expensive to be viable.

Do you think dancers are respected?

Dancers never get respect. I think it's incredibly sad, I wish I could do something about that. Dancers have a vocation – they're dedicated and trained in their profession, they just don't get the reverence they deserve. They should have more respect and I hate the way dancers are brushed under the carpet. Even when Pan's People were at the height of their fame the BBC would not recognise us as a group; we were paid as 'the dancers' and contracted as 'the dancers' individually.

How long was your professional dancing career?

The last dancing performance I did was in 1996, so 33 years.

As well as a successful dancing career you launched The Dance Attic Studios. How did that come about and how did it become so well-known?

In 1981 I started the Dance Attic actually in a small attic room. It actually belonged to Roger Waters of Pink Floyd. When it expanded we moved to Putney, then in 1992 to The Old Fulham Baths and the name always stuck.

It got a reputation for being reliable and cheap and cheerful. We have never advertised and it has grown purely by word of mouth and reputation. We kept our prices very realistic and during the recession when other companies were falling like flies, we didn't, and everybody came and rehearsed here – Anthony Hopkins, Mick Jagger, Andrew Lloyd Webber. Now all today's pop stars come too, like Boyzone, 911, Eternal, Robbie Williams and Vanessa Mae.

What is there in the Dance Attic for dancers?

Dance classes, singing lessons, studios and rehearsal rooms, a coffee bar, a gym, a dancewear shop, a dance agency and a theatre. It's a good place to make contacts and rub shoulders with some famous performers. The Dance Attic is one of two or three places in London a dancer needs to know about. I'm very proud of it!

Dancers from 'X-Directory'

PHOTO: SERGIO BONDIONI

The girls tell it as it is

Harriet *from Manchester (5ft 9in) began dancing at the age of one and trained at Bush Davis. Her credits include a Diana Ross TV Special in Madrid, a live performance by The Supremes in Berlin, live stage productions in Italy, Portugal and on Caribbean cruises, and Gala shows for The Moulin Rouge, Paris.*

It wasn't really my childhood dream to become a dancer, more a case of something that just progressed from a hobby. I didn't really know what attracted me to dancing at that young age, I just knew I used to enjoy it. My mother is heavily involved in dance but she wasn't one of these pushy mothers by any means. She wanted me to do what I wanted to do. It was my decision to dance. Having said that, she was a big influence. As soon as I could walk I used to go and watch her teach. I actually trained in ballet and athletics and I used to compete, then I moved on to horse riding. By the age of 12 I had to give up athletics and riding because I was developing quadriceps. I build muscle really easily. I carried on with my dancing. My mum used to train Arlene Phillips so I went to Pineapple when I was young and I thought it was the most brilliant, most fascinating place to be. She danced with The Royal Ballet Company for a while and worked with George Formby and did a lot of cabaret in Blackpool. Mum was highly trained as well – advanced RAD. She trained me until I was about 11, then I reached a point when I didn't want her to teach me and I moved to another teacher. I nearly went away to The Hammond Boarding Ballet school in Chester at 11, but my parents decided against it because vocational schools suffer academically. I auditioned for The Royal who said they would accept me after 12 months full-time classical training (I wasn't strong enough after dancing just once a week after school), so I got into Bush Davis College at 16 and ended up staying there for three years instead of going to The Royal. I had discovered jazz and tap and made friends.

I think I was quite sheltered at college, they didn't really tell us what was going on in the real world back then. It was very ballet-oriented and if you weren't Ballet Company material they sort of looked down on you. Big snobbery! No-one prepared us for work really, except for presentation classes in the third year with a woman who skimmed over how to do a CV and talked about photography. Basically she told us nothing! I couldn't be a professional classical dancer because I stress-fractured both tibias and suffered from shin splints. If I really wanted to I could have been chosen for a German classical company, but I had too much time off and all I really wanted to do was commercial dancing in London; I only ended up abroad so much to get my Equity card! After that I moved to London to dance.

I've covered all kinds of work over the years, from showgirl stuff to 'Do It All' ads. I've been lucky enough to appear in quite a few TV commercials. I seem to have the face for them and they are well paid which helps! My first job was quite hysterical. There was this woman who set up some kind of an agency in connection with college, for dancers to work and get their Equity cards. She got a group of us, boys and girls (some really talented people), a job touring round Italy with an eccentric guy called Guy Stranger and his girlfriend who used to dance nude adagio along with a French band and a really famous Accordion player who later turned out to be part of the mafia mob. Off we went touring in a 1930s bus that went about 30 miles per hour. We spent a few nights sleeping (or trying to) in the bus and we travelled 5,000 miles in one month. We rehearsed in a seedy barn beside an empty swimming pool outside Bari with the choreographer teaching us a Can Can like you wouldn't believe. Then we had TV cameras following us around and we found out we had to wear g-strings with underwired bras, with only tiny diamanté circles covering our nipples! We were just out of college and thought we were going to be ballet dancers in a big commercial TV gala. In Italy they call their gala shows 'Ballets' and the dancers 'les Ballerinas' so we were completely misled. After a week of rehearsals we had a costume fitting and all freaked out saying, 'We want to go home!' All because some woman told us she would get us our Equity card! (I do actually get to use my Equity card; I always have to write my number on consent forms for TV commercial work.)

To be a showgirl you need to be tall and loose, it's basically just parading around. Flexibility is important, you need to be a high kicker and have a good physique. The routines aren't very taxing except for some of the kicklines. We did a lot of stuff like Japanese numbers with kimonos and fans, and Egyptian numbers. All the costumes were amazing. I remember once dancing to this shocking 70s wah wah music and we had to be air hostesses. We wore beautiful little blue jackets with g-strings, 5in silver shoes and a little briefcase which had a letter that spelled out the name of the showbar. Once I did a gala show at The Moulin Rouge in Paris which was hysterical. I had two days to learn 22 numbers amongst about 20 temperamental French male and female dancers who were resident there. We had to wear jewellery, feathers, different outfits, matching gloves. It was really hard work. There was a huge finale with a fountain centre stage and staircases cascading down either side with big pillars and statues, all very decadent and elaborate. We were supposed to drape ourselves down from this cascading staircase wearing white bikinis with huge feathers and jewels, but we had to dress ourselves and it was really difficult. We had no help and the costumes were heavy and one girl shouted out in the costume change 'What do I wear?' The French girls didn't reply, so she ended up in this beautiful finale with black gloves on with green feathers! She managed the white bikini though! The choreographer was stood in the wings going absolutely crazy, shouting all sorts in French and telling the girl to get off stage. It was so funny it totally ruined the finale!

I also did a six-month contract in the Algarve in the Vilamoura Casino which was a large cabaret show. It was quite funky with lots of *pas de deux*. I did a very classical Spanish Adagio – I broke a rib doing it one evening! We had two guys with us and we did eight or nine numbers with lots of quick changes. The show was given in the restaurant so the guests had dinner then watched the gala show.

I've done quite a few cruises too (to get my full Equity). I saw an ad in *The Stage* for a Caribbean cruise audition one day and I thought I'd love to do that! I'm so chuffed I did it, I went everywhere – Mexico, the Virgin Islands. I think every dancer should travel at the start of their career. It opens your eyes to the rest of the world and helps you grow up. I think it grounds you as a person. It's cabaret and I found the dancing quite limited although we did a fab *42nd Street* tap routine. The social aspect was great for me. I'd just recommend it. You do about one duty every two days (welcoming guests on and off the ship). I shared a cabin with another dancer (the head girl) and we all worked as a close team and became real friends. I had a brilliant time. The money is alright too – everything was paid for, your accommodation, your food and you had a weekly wage which was basically spending money. Great for a young dancer.

When I came back from dancing on cruises I decided to move to London and I didn't know any agents – who was good, who wasn't. So I used to hang around Pineapple Studios in Covent Garden, talk to other dancers, get addresses and then contact them. My favourite commercial job so far was probably dancing at Wembley Stadium. I've also choreographed lots of PA tours and live dancing gigs. I've just passed my associate diploma which qualifies me to enter dancers for major ISTD (The Imperial Society of Teachers of Dancing) exams, so I'm fully qualified to teach dance and I have a couple of jobs in schools around London which fits in with my freelance dancing. I have been a dancer for ten years and now I regularly work as a backing singer mostly round Europe for a German agent. I have also recently moved into presenting, which is the part of my career I would like to do more of as I get older and more experienced.

Lisa *from London (5ft 7in) began dancing at the age of four and trained at Arts Educational. Her credits include UK tours with Take That, Steve Coogan and E17, world tours with Gina G and Cathy Dennis and TV appearances on The MTV Awards,* Smash Hits *Party and The Brit Awards.*

I began dance lessons at a local dance school. I did ballet, tap and modern then started ballet classes on Saturdays at 'The Dance Centre'. My teacher thought I had the potential to audition for The Royal Ballet (junior associates) so I had some private lessons, auditioned and was accepted. I went there twice a week for two years. I then went to Arts Educational from the age of 11 to 16, followed by two years as a student. I knew I wasn't going to be a classical dancer by the time I was a student (even though that was my original aim), because so much pressure was put on me from about the age of 15 to lose weight. They wanted me to look a certain shape and I realised I could do more commercial dance without so much pressure on my size.

I was going to give up dancing and do a secretarial course if it hadn't been for a friend of mine at college called Kevan Allen (choreographer) who asked me to join a dance group he'd formed. You do need to be slim to dance, but not minute and when I left college and started working I realised it was not the most important thing. When I left college I used to do two classes a day but it got too expensive so I joined a gym where I do a couple of workouts a week or aerobics three times a week. I also train in Kung-Fu. It all sounds impressive but when I'm working there's no time for training.

My first job was with a group called Beauxartz, supporting Bucks Fizz at a nightclub in Watford! I've done a couple of Royal Variety shows, but the most exciting job for me was the Take That tour in '95. Most audiences held about 15,000 people – it was a great adrenalin rush! Kim Gavin was the choreographer. There were long rehearsals but the end reward was worth it. A dancer straight from college would be able to cope with a job on that scale, but only if they were confident in their ability and streetwise. It's a lot of pressure handling the nerves and working with very experienced people. I've done a couple of world tours with different pop artistes which has taken me to most places. It is definitely a perk of the job, although sometimes you don't get to see much more than the inside of a TV studio or hotel. However, with most artistes you are free to explore and drink cocktails while they do all their interviews and promotion. One of the funniest jobs I have done was being dressed as a lettuce leaf with a slice of cucumber on my head and green stiletto shoes for a salad dressing commercial!

I have about eight agents, four of which I work through all the time. I do audition for work but I also get work through recommendation. Generally for the big tours there is always an audition. Although I have a CV and photo I don't always hand out my CV unless I'm asked. I usually just give a photo.

I sometimes find it difficult getting back on to 'the scene' when I have been on tour for long periods. I do work consistently though. I think you can make a decent living from dancing, but there's always that thing of saving money for a rainy day if you don't work for a month. If you have a face for TV commercials you can make a lot of money, but they are few and far between. If you can work for bands, do fashion shows and trade shows you will earn a decent living. I think there is a pool of about 30–40 top 'commercial' dancers in London who work all the time; I'd say just less than half of those are male. It's a little easier for guys because there's fewer of them in the business, especially *good* ones. When dancers are in a production they are taken for granted, but if you took them out of the picture, *that's* when people notice. No-one appreciates how hard it is to dance unless they actually try to do it. Then again we are paid to make it look easy.

Jazz used to be very classically based, but now it's more street style. The more skills you have like acrobatics, tap, break dancing, the more chances you have of getting work.

I think colleges should allow students to go out and audition, because otherwise when you leave you haven't got a clue what to wear or how to pick up the different choreographers' styles. They should invite guest choreographers into college classes. You don't get told what it's like out there when you're training. Some colleges are turning out dancers of a good enough standard but there's only a few that make it through. You will work by being a good dancer, but it's also how you look and your attitude. If people can rely on you and know you will turn up on time and not back chat or cause problems, it counts for a lot. There is a lot of politics between agents, choreographers and dancers, and you need to ignore it and stay focused, otherwise you end up trying to please everyone other than yourself.

I think a lot of dancers are insecure because of all the rejection involved. It's easy to start blaming yourself and just eat yourself up. It can be a bitchy business sometimes, but you just have to let it go. You can't get bitter and twisted over jobs you didn't get, because it doesn't get you anywhere and backstabbing other dancers will end your career in no time (news travels fast). Dancers have been bitchy to my face in the past and it does hurt, but you have to try and ignore it. You have to learn how to play the game, especially when you're fresh out of college.

I'm proud of what I've done. I can look back on a few nightmare jobs, but it's all part of gaining experience. It's a fun job, there's a good side to it, travelling and socialising, but you have to be able to cope with the good and the bad. I've been a commercial dancer for 14 years now and I think I've covered everything. I'm still enjoying it but I can't do it forever. I'm doing a computer course at the moment and would eventually like to work in a record company. There is also the question of children in a year or two, so I will call it a day then.

Charlotte *from Surrey (5ft 7in) began dancing at the age of two and trained at Corona Academy. Her credits include TV appearances on* The Clothes Show, Gladiators, Top Of The Pops, The Brit Awards *and* The National Lottery Show. *She was also assistant choreographer for the E17 world tour and has participated in further world tours dancing with Whigfield and Alex Party.*

I began dancing at the age of two; my sister went to a local dancing school and I wanted to do everything she did. I went to a stage school at 12 called the Corona Academy, it's now known as the Ravenscourt Park Theatre School. At 16 I was offered a job dancing in the West End so I jacked in all the academic exams I should have taken, had a battle with my parents and took the job. I regret not taking my school exams, because although I've never needed them I wish I had them now to help me give up dancing after 12 years and change my career. I think they would give me a lot more confidence and back me up on paper. The public assume we're all thick because we use our legs, not our brain. They are so wrong, we use our brain just as much as our body, if not more! If I had some academic qualifications it would boost my confidence. Support from your family is very important. I think dancers should have a basic strategy and know what direction they want to go in and have something they can fall back on. Having back-up will give you confidence throughout your career, especially after the rejections.

My dad got me my schedule D number and I use his accountant, but I didn't have a clue about income tax as a self-employed dancer, nobody tells you what to do. You need to be aware and ask questions.

When I started out there used to be huge open auditions for jobs like Summertime Special, but now it's so rare to see auditions that everyone goes along and it's mayhem. The sad thing is, the client may be using it as a publicity stunt for a band or for his own ego and they may only need one or two dancers out of the 100 auditioning. Dancers are turned away feeling totally deflated, but that's the way to start learning about the industry. You will be let down time and time again. Even when you are working regularly and earning good money you will average at least one knock-back a month. You must learn to deal with it each time and get used to them. Some dancers don't and that makes for an insecure and sometimes bitter dancer, they wallow in negative energy and this rubs off on others which is when it can become bitchy.

To be a successful commercial dancer you are looking at being between 5ft 6in and 5ft 8in, good-looking and confident. You have to be competitive in this industry because there's so many people that want to do it and not enough jobs for them all.

Dancing is a glamorous career and there are some fantastic moments in-between the hard work. You may not realise it at the time. I've been in limousines, flown across the world first class, seen some amazing countries and been treated very well at hotels. Another career might not have given me those experiences. So yes it can be very glamorous – this makes up for the amount of let downs you experience! But I hate the hype in London about the way you need to look and how you should speak to be seen as a cool commercial dancer.

I have about seven agents, but I rely on my own contacts for work. The majority of my work has been commercial dancing – hair shows, pop stuff. When I became successful and got tons of castings I probably got one job in every five auditions, and there came a time when I didn't even *need* to audition. I went from job to job. Then I went away for a while and on my return getting my foot back in the door was hard work.

The most entertaining of jobs have to have been the Army tours, travelling to the most unusual places around the world with my best friends to dance in front of crowds of men! I have fired a machine gun, driven a tank and flown in a Hercules, never mind sitting in the ejector seat of a Tornado! I've met the most interesting people and made some very close friends. Another really enjoyable job I have done was when I went to Japan to do a hair show with a choreographer named Kevan Allen. He is the best this country has seen. He had carefully calculated how to choose 29 dancers who would all get on, work with each other and support each other and do the most outrageous hours, being pushed and pulled about all day having their hair done and showing the styles while dancing out the show – it was fabulous and we had the most fantastic time. It was an accumulation of all the well-known West End shows put together and every dancer had their own solo to do. She would start a number and show the hair style, but it was so well thought out. The choreographer had planned the style of dance to go with the hair style which was a 90s style, but depicted from say the 1920s and so that style of dance was reflected in the choreography. It was clever. It was one of my most enjoyable jobs and one of the most arduous.

Yes, I want children and a house – a dancing career is short-lived. As for moving on and changing careers, my advice to dancers trying to give up is that you may be able to approach one of the companies you've danced for and got to know on a personal level and apply for a non-dancing position. But be aware that they may remember you as their backing dancer and have no faith in you sat behind a desk in the accounts department, so find a way of proving yourself on paper when you apply for the job.

Michelle *from Gloucestershire (5ft 7in) began dancing at eight years of age and trained at Laine Theatre Arts. Her credits include appearing in videos and on live shows for Boyzone, E17, Ant & Dec, Whigfield, 911 and Five. She's also participated in a world tour with Gina G and appeared on* Top Of The Pops, The Generation Game, The Royal Variety Show, MTV Awards *and* The Brit Awards.

I went to a local dancing school first and then full-time dance training at Laine Theatre Arts at the age of 16. I did get a grant, well I got my fees paid but not my maintenance. I was lucky, my parents never forced me into anything and I ended up with 7 O levels. I didn't do A levels but went straight to dance college instead. My parents knew that's what I wanted to do at the time and they were just happy that I was able to pursue it. The fact that I passed the audition for college meant that they knew I was serious as they are difficult to get in to. They said if I came out of college and got one good dancing job then they knew it was all worthwhile – they only told me that recently and now they're chuffed because I've managed to make money from dancing.

My first job was in Italy for six weeks. It was a topless show and I was one of the only two dressed dancers there. I did it to get my Equity card, but I was swindled out of it which was a pretty bad start to my career. It hardly made me feel like I had become a fully professional dancer, and I even gave up for four months – I hated it! I thought I was useless and couldn't dance any more. Then I contacted my college who advised me to write a threatening letter to the choreographer and I was eventually given an Equity card. This enabled me to do a summer season for Michael Barrymore. Alan Harding choreographed it and I loved it – this was the proper start to my career. The funny part is I've hardly used my Equity card, seeing as most of the work I've done hasn't been Equity contracts. Nowadays you don't need one as much as you used to.

I've never wanted to be famous. My main career goal was just to be a successful dancer. You can make a very good living as a dancer. In London where I live there's about 50 dancers who make an excellent living; then maybe about 150 who earn a fair living, then the rest get by. But every dancer has to take the good with the bad. Dancing is not as glamorous as it sounds – people tend to think you're completely thick! They are shallow enough to assume you have no brains because you wear skimpy clothes, do a physical job and grin like a Cheshire cat when you're working. Although there are glamorous moments, it's mainly hard work. As for a dancer's height, everyone's always lying. You need to say you're at least 5ft 7in or over. If you're 5ft 8in you'll never stop working as a commercial dancer – you can do fashion or trade shows and earn excellent money. If you're anything under you'll always have a bit of a problem although it's not impossible. For

TV shows it doesn't really matter how tall you are as long as you're good. I do go down the gym, and I do have to work at keeping my body trim. When I give up I will inevitably become bigger, but the fact that I won't have to wear hot pants any more will help – as long as I look decent in everyday clothes. I'll never stop exercising though as my joints would seize up. I do diet sometimes, not massively, but I have to watch what I eat.

The most unusual commercial casting I've done was in London when we were asked to shout out *'prawn!'* in Italian and dance around like a prawn, then shout out *'tomato!'* and *'salad!'* and dance like a salad. I got the job as a dancing lettuce leaf! It was filmed in Italy and I was the only English speaking person on the whole set which was quite amusing as I couldn't understand any of the directions. The worst costume I've ever had to dance in was a fluorescent leotard! The best dancing job has got to be the MTV awards, which was probably the most prestigious.

I have five agents but I also rely on my friends and my own contacts for work and I choreograph a bit. I'm assisting a choreographer at the moment. I've never got any jobs from entering my photo into a casting book. I have always got my work through my dancing talent or meeting and talking to someone face to face. I don't often get work from having my face on a bit of cardboard. I still think it's important for dancers to have photographs though as some dancers get all their work from their Z card, especially the commercial dancing jobs. If your picture is excellent and you're with the agency that's right for you, then it's definitely worthwhile for dancers to go into casting books or on a website page, and it's also a tax deductible expense! But if you're not particularly photogenic like me then there's no point. I know if I was a client looking through a book then I wouldn't choose me! You just end up on a page between stunning people who have a great look on paper, and if the client's not looking for someone stunning then they would probably go to a character agency anyway. You also have to be careful you don't pay out to go in lots of agencies' books – it gets very expensive and some of them will just be sent to the same clients so you have to think it through.

As I get older I don't find it more difficult to get work, quite the opposite. People like to use older dancers, not because they're any better than the younger girls but because they have more experience. They know you're not going to mess up, they can send dancers out with just one day's rehearsal and know they will look wicked, instead of sending dancers out there not knowing and thinking 'Oh my God I hope they pull it off'. You mustn't get disheartened when you start out, as most choreographers like using the same people because they know they are reliable. I've no age limit as to when I'll give up dancing. If the work keeps coming in I'll do it, if it dries up all together and an opportunity arises then I'll do something else. When I've retired from dancing I'll probably do something in production, putting on events or in the recording industry. I've worked for all these types of company and I feel like I know how they operate. If I sat down now and made a list of all my contacts and wrote to them I could probably get myself a non-dancing job. So when I've finished being in the limelight I will probably do something behind the scenes.

Lisa *from Vancouver, Canada (5ft 6in) began dancing at the age of three and trained at Royal Winnipeg Ballet School, Goh Ballet Academy and The Edge, LA. Her credits include the West End musical* Chicago, *shows* What A Feeling, West Side Story, *videos for Salt n' Pepa and Coolio, choreography for Louise and Kavana.*

I started dancing when I was four or five years old and when I was about 12 I took it more seriously, doing ballet every day. I used to watch Baryshnikov and Janet Jackson and I aspired to be like them or at least one of their dancers, so me and my friends headed in that direction. I started doing professional gigs when I was very young. I was fortunate enough to get on a TV series called the *Green Double Decker Show* – my uncle was a producer on it and got me a 'go see' (casting) and that helped me to network and find out about other work. We didn't have any full-time colleges in Canada, we only had part-time 'dance schools'. I went to Miss Jasmin Gardener School of Dance and then Valerie Eastern School of Dance. There we did a lot of competitions and she had a great reputation for producing good dancers who won all the trophies.

Becoming a choreographer happened through my teaching. I went to my regular class and one day the teacher let me take the class because she was going to be late. I liked it, and then I started teaching little kids at another studio and gradually built up more classes. Then I found a studio which I began to lease and it blossomed into a school for about eight years. We had 24 classes a week with five teachers. I formed a company called Body Electric and we used to do gigs around the city – Expo 86 in Vancouver and so many jobs for all kinds of industrial companies. In Vancouver the business is really building – it's like North Hollywood. There's a lot of musical theatre going on there, *The X-files* is filmed there, *Millennium* was filmed there, so there's tons of work.

I love performing too much to go home though. Back there I was just doing choreography and working with my dance company, Vancouver Dance Force. I think there's more for me to pursue here. I'm playing Annie in *Chicago* in the West End at the moment, which is fulfilling one of my ambitions. Also I've choreographed for Kavana and Louise and I've made contacts, so I really want to pursue my choreography in London. I only have one agent at the moment, but I may explore a few other avenues soon. In Vancouver they encourage you to get into auditions right away so you can get used to the nerves and so people get to know your face. They emphasise the fun and the love of dance much more, whereas here in London the kids aren't really allowed to audition while they're in college. I think it's great that they start the kids so young here in a competitive environment, there are so many colleges and they concentrate on all aspects of dance and drama and singing, but it has drawbacks like not letting the kids out into the industry soon enough so they don't always know what to expect.

Although jazz taught in college is not really what you see in pop videos, I think you need the jazz technique and the strength to be able to apply different styles. It's essential for a good jazz technique to be taught in a dancer's training whether it's Matt Mattox, Cunningham etc. Doing street jazz is a matter of going into class and picking up the style. I've always based my style on Bob Fosse and I think a lot of street jazz is just a mixture of techniques and styles. I teach 'Street Slammin' which is a good example of this. It's street jazz with edge – I use the word 'slammin' to try and describe the cool style.

I've worked in Vegas for Madonna's *Erotica* CD launch with Oliver Coombes, one of the Girlie tour backing dancers, Coolio and Bryan Adams. I think once you get to a certain level meeting other people in the industry is the fun bit. I danced a lot in LA and I wanted to go to New York, but then I decided London had more character and history and the whole business here is more funky! New York is very sophisticated. I go to LA every summer and take classes at a place called The Edge in West Hollywood. You pass by Janet Jackson and Alicia Silverstone taking class so it's a good place to be seen. I have a lot of friends that dance for Janet, but I don't have a green card so I only get work out there that goes under the table, like working with Salt 'n' Pepa and Spinderella. Tina Landon (Janet Jackson's choreographer) and Bob Fosse are the two major influences on my choreography.

How do I choose my dancers? Well I'll be auditioning for Kavana's tour next year and I'm really looking for people who can pick up the style. I teach for a company called Global Vibrations where teachers come to London from around the world and teach class in workshops and show styles that are new here. I do the jazz and Adam Garcia from *Saturday Night Fever* does the tap. The classes are packed and real fun. You need to get on the mailing list to hear about the classes. I see some really good dancers there and sometimes take their number to bear them in mind for future work. I think it's important to 'hang out' at dance studios even if you're not a schmoozy type of person, which I'm not. My mother always told me – you have to be able to be nice to everybody, because if you're a snob and you have a 'chip' on your shoulder nobody wants to hire you. Whenever I'm auditioning and I see someone with a bad attitude I think, well they've gotta work with the other dancers for weeks on end and I don't want to hire someone that thinks they're so great. So you need to be within certain circles and be likeable, but at the same time try and find out information – what auditions are happening, who's choreographing, what are your friends up to.

Chapter Thirteen

The Male Dancer

Almost all of the information in this book is also relevant to male dancers. Male dancers certainly have as many hurdles to jump in their career as female dancers. The same rules apply to boys as they do to girls with regards to height and looks for certain commercial jobs – sometimes you are too small or your face doesn't fit. There is no easy way in just because you are male. The process of training, auditioning, getting noticed, getting work and getting paid remains the same. Your priorities must be to dance very well, look fantastic and be confident. Despite the fact that there are less boys than girls, it doesn't affect the high standard of dancing expected to get good work. Male dancers have to be fit and very strong. They cannot get away with anything less. They have to show dynamics in their dancing and have strength and judgment to lift dancers. Fit and toned bodies are also important. Often male costumes are simple designs that need great bodies in them to come alive. Attention must be paid to your looks and styling when looking for work. The male dancer with a spotty face and floppy hair is not presentable. You don't need to apply full make-up for auditions but spot cover-up and hair gel can work wonders whatever sex you are!

There are not as many guys out there as there are girls and for some reason this makes people assume that it is far easier for male dancers to get work. In fact it is no different because the ratio of jobs for male dancers is equivalent to that of female dancers. For example, if a male dancer applies for a summer season and he attends an audition of 60 girls and just 20 boys, it may appear that his chances are greater but the client wants to find six girls and just two boys, so it is all relative. Some jobs are also unsuitable for male dancers, which narrows down their chances of work even more.

The advantages of being a male dancer are during audition time. Although the initial 'cattle market' moment with all the dancers squashed together trying to pick up a routine is the same, the boys normally get a good chance when they are grouped together to audition because suddenly they have space! They have the undivided attention of the auditioners because there are usually so few of them compared to the girls and they seem to be nicely spread out and easy to watch. This also means mistakes are easily spotted, however.

If you are a reliable, talented male dancer you can gain a good reputation. Providing you approach the industry wisely and make the

PHOTO: ERIK BERG/ARENA IMAGES

effort to build a good relationship with your agents and choreographers, it's surprising how often you'll be asked to dance without the need to audition. It can take a shorter period of time for outstanding male dancers to be remembered by clients due to the reduced number of them in comparison to girls. However no-one likes to work with a dancer with a bad attitude, male or female, no matter how talented they are.

Commercial male dancers must also keep up with the trends. Image is an important element in commercial work. Spiky hair and combat trousers; long hair in a pony tail and cropped tops; dungarees and open shirts; bald heads – all these fashions reached the dance floor and it's important to be aware of the look for now. A strong technique alongside a strong image will help you stand out. Musical theatre work, on the other hand, relies more on the male dancers who sing and are less interested in their hair style. If your dancing is sound and you sing confidently and 'in tune' it is usually enough.

There are no special guidelines for males in the dancing industry; it may be predominately female but all dancers need the dedication and determination to achieve their goals and a positive attitude to steer them on their way.

Lyndon *from London began dancing at the age of twelve and trained at Italia Conti. His credits include choreography for The Lighthouse Family, All Saints, Umboza and Strike and dancing on* Top Of The Pops, The Pepsi Chart Show, *MTV and* The Big Breakfast.

I manage a career as a dancer and choreographer, and this is only difficult when people get confused between the two. I trained to be a dancer first, going to Italia Conti when I was 13 and asked to leave at 17 because I got a job via the school agency which the school wanted me to turn down. It was for a boy band and I took the job, but it was about 1985 before boy bands made it big so it flopped. Before that I went to a local dance school in Esher. I began acting first then started dancing at the age of 12. I got involved in a lot of productions like *Oliver* where we had to do both. I also got involved in disco dancing, doing competitions, which is brilliant training for a commercial dancer, and making up routines. Great grounding. I don't really dance any more. I sometimes used to dance as well as choreograph to save a client money or to pad out a show, but I don't need the credits on my CV any more. I've choreographed for about six years now, with 13 years as a dancer. The boy band was my first job, but after that flopped I was lucky enough to land three big commercials and earn a lot of money. I remember thinking – this is easy, why does everybody say I'm going to struggle, but then I didn't work for about six months! I even had to work front of house for the Dominion Theatre for a bit.

I don't think it's easier for male dancers to get work. A lot of people think it is, but there are as many good boys as there are girls and usually clients don't need as many boy dancers for jobs. There's maybe three girls and just one boy booked, for example.

I choreograph all sorts of stuff. I do lots of hair shows and conferences and pop promos. The reason I became a choreographer was because I wasn't being fulfilled as a dancer. A lot of the choreography just wasn't up to date and I thought I could do better. I could see a bigger picture. A choreographer's job can be anything from getting two backing singers to look good behind an act, to staging 90 kids in a musical number. It is basically to create suitable movement. I think the secret of being a good choreographer is to get a good performance out of a dancer. I usually hear a track and a load of ideas come from just listening to the music. Dance music is my main inspiration, and I use instrumental dance tracks when I can. I'll be in a club and hear music or an artiste I'd like to work with. I begin to see steps to go with a song, then I'll get my agent to chase the track to see if they need a choreographer. I have one agent for choreography and one for photographic work. I used to have tons and they all got me bits and pieces, but now I'm of an age where I just need one agent to focus on my work. Choreographing can pay well and should be paid well. We get paid much more than dancers because we've got so much more work to do. All the dancers are doing is working during the rehearsal time. With choreography, the preparation involved and the whole concept involves a lot more pre-production than you imagine, plus you are there to sort out all the dancers' problems, from injuries to costumes and sometimes personal traumas. Choreographers have a longer career than dancers because they can still do it when they're not so young and beautiful. For publicity a choreographer needs showreels. It's as important as a photo and CV for a dancer. The trouble is you need the work to make a showreel. In the beginning I just plagued companies for work and kept calling them until they gave me a chance. Eventually I want to go on to direct pop videos. I've started directing on some of my jobs as a choreographer and I can see myself doing more of that as I get older. I've got so many ideas – I'm hungry for it all which is a very important quality in this industry.

Has a client ever hated my work? I haven't had that happen to me yet. Sometimes they comment on certain steps, but if they are paying me to do a job I will listen to constructive criticism and sort it out with them. We usually reach a compromise. It can be awkward choreographing for TV shows if you choreograph stuff specifically for the given camera angles and then they don't shoot that part. Cameramen have a great knack of missing all the creative patterns choreographers work so hard to create. The strangest thing I've been asked to create was four tap routines in four inches of water for a Chinese laser show in a theme park.

They wanted to recreate Fred and Ginger superimposed on to a 60ft fountain.

If I want to book dancers I normally use my agent or I call the dancers up as well and tell them to talk to my agent for more details. I hold auditions for a client or agent if I'm asked. I don't go for a particular look, it really depends on what my client is looking for. The way to get to know choreographers is through the agencies or by going along to classes. I tend to stick to dancers I know for pieces I choreograph, which is bad but it is so much easier if you can use people who know how I operate, especially if there is little time to get a job done. I do use a new dancer if she comes with a recommendation or really stands out at an audition. The advice I'd give to a dancer who was about to audition for me would be – don't be false. It's really easy to see false people, you can really tell. And do work your way to the front, do show yourself off. I try to look at the back row but you can be easily missed.

David *from London began dancing at the age of 14 and trained at Stella Mann School of Ballet. His credits include West End musicals* Fame, Cats, Copacabana, *a tour of* An Evening with Tommy Steele, *and TV appearances on* Top Of The Pops.

I started off wanting to be an actor and went to The Royal Court Young People's Theatre Group in Sloane Square at the age of 14 for two years. It hadn't crossed my mind to be a dancer until I became inspired by the film *Fame*. Also there was a documentary on television called 'Bring On The Dancing Girls' and there was a feature on a group called 'Spinooch' who were a spin off from Hot Gossip and basically it was about their lives and how they prepared for gigs. I thought 'Yeah that looks really good'. Because of *Fame* I really wanted to do musicals. First of all I went on a foundation course at South East London College. The first time I had ever danced was at the audition and it just felt really natural. We had percussionists and a drummer and I just followed, so I got accepted and spent a year there. Then I went to The Laban Centre and studied contemporary dance for a short period and then I left there because I found it too theoretical and more aimed at teaching, which was not what I wanted to do.

Dance groups were big at the time. It was the middle-80s and I auditioned for Hot Gossip and Arlene Phillips really liked me, but she wanted me to finish my training so she took me on as an understudy which became a kind of summer job for me. I never actually got to do a performance or get paid but it was great experience. I was going on 17 and rehearsing at Pineapple and hanging out and getting into the feel of it all. Then I went to Stella Mann School of Ballet. From there I had to finish my studies early because I got picked to do *The Pajama Game* for the Leicester Haymarket production which was my first professional job. I was one of the steam heat boys which was great.

I've just finished dancing in the musical *Fame* and shortly begin rehearsals for *Oh What A Night*. I will be dancing for Kim Gavin which I'm looking forward to, because he is one of the big choreographers in the country. I understudied Tyrone in *Fame* and I got to go on and play him in London at the Cambridge Theatre, and subsequently on tour. The first big part I played was Richie in *A Chorus Line*. I remember auditioning for that, it was just manic. There were 3,000 people for about 17 parts! It was literally like the film. There were some fantastic people who went up for it, so it was a real honour when they offered me the part of Richie. It was such a buzz! It was directed by Baayork Lee who was the original Connie Wong, she's the only woman who has permission from The Michael Bennett Estate to put on *A Chorus Line* all over the world. I was asked to play the same role in Italy, but because of other work commitments, I had to decline. I played Swing in *Cats* for two years, and it took me a year to get it together, it was a nightmare to learn. Then I did the show again with choreographer Gillian Lynne and director Trevor Nunn when it was revamped and I played Coricopat, one of the mystical twins. I did the *Cats* audition four times before I actually got in. I always got through to the final, but was always told the part they had me in mind for wasn't available. For the audition we would dance first, then we'd be called back in the afternoon on the same day to sing and then be recalled on a different day to do the same thing all again. For musical theatre you can end up doing endless recalls. There were 40 boys at my final recall and I was the only one they chose. It's steady income doing a musical, you get contracted for a year.

Boy dancers aren't treated any different to girl dancers. For musical auditions you usually have boys on one day then girls on another, and for commercial jobs you are all together, but it's no different. If you are good you will stand out – it's as simple as that. For commercial stuff looks are definitely important, not so much for musicals. That's more technique, and singing is one of the fundamental things. It really annoys me when dancers say 'I can't sing' but they'd love to do musicals. Everyone can sing! It's all about finding the right song, finding the right key, and finding the right teacher, that's all it is.

Rehearsal periods for musicals are about four weeks and they are fun I think because it's something that's being created or restaged and you become like a family. You bond with people in the cast. You work very closely together for a long time so attachments are made. You have to get along and if you have a quarrel it has to be dismissed the minute you get on stage. You can't take it with you. Mentally and physically it can be draining because you are doing the same thing for eight shows a week plus extra rehearsals. It takes a strong discipline to be able to cope with it. Sometimes there are rehearsals during the week, like clean up calls or understudy rehearsals.

I've been professional 14 years and I've been dancing all the time. If there has been two or three months without much going on I have gone out and found work or gone abroad. I worked in Greece for seven months in the sunshine. It was one of my best jobs, it had such a good working atmosphere I loved it. People watching dancers just see the glamour of it all, hopping from one show to the next. They don't realise the discipline and training involved before you get anywhere. We work really hard but people just think we're getting paid for doing what we enjoy. Not everyone is successful and it is a difficult career. You have got to have confidence to make it as a dancer. You have got to believe you can do it and be able to prove it on the day. It's important to be able to adjust to different styles as well. It's a good idea to do professional classes for experience. I still like doing classes. I love keeping fit and stretched. I started doing classes at Pineapple as well as going to college and trained under a woman called Libby Rose on and off for about eight years. Now I do class about four times a week if I'm in a show and if I'm not then I'll do a class every day. Global Vibrations is the best thing to happen to jazz dance in Britain for years. It took an American girl called Ariadni to come over and change things. You have a wide choice of classes: you can get strong technical jazz teachers, funky jazz teachers – it gives a whole range with an American flavour. There are still the contemporary jazz teachers like Stuart Arnold and Paul Henry, who are great teachers but more technical, which I think is good. Also Dolly Henry, who teaches a dynamic form of technical jazz and has her own company called 'Bop' (whom I occasionally perform with). So many teachers just teach a funky style, which is cool, but there is more to it than just being funky. Technique went down a hell of a lot when the funky street style was introduced. Everyone was aiming towards that style and one day a teacher would ask for a develope layout and dancers would freak because they had limited themselves to just hip hop jazz. You can't do that. Dance is a whole world of different movements. It's important to be versatile and not limit yourself to just one style of dance.

The dance industry has gone through a change. During the 80s there was a huge amount of work, loads of videos and commercials, and dancing seemed much more competitive. Then the work went down a bit and dancers weren't used as much. I don't think they had the money to spend on us. They got models who looked good to do all the videos and just sway around a bit. Now I think it's back, what with all the break dancing, body-popping and Irish dancing.

I belong to the main dance agencies, but I also have personal management now. I get auditions via my agents or by word of mouth. I get a lot of work on my own. People call me up, especially if I have worked for them before and they like my work. I do all kinds of stuff. I have been a telly dancer, I've worked for Jeff Richer and Brian Rogers, and I've branched out in all different styles of dance. I like doing commercial work because it's short and well paid! Unfortunately you have to do the business side to your career too. You have to find a good accountant. My accountant specialises in dancers and looks after 343 of us. It's tedious and boring and you can neglect it, but you have got to do it eventually by law. You have to list everything you spend and everything you earn.

I've trained as a yoga teacher. I read a book called *Wake up to Yoga* and I tried it and it was great, it really helped me, I liked it a lot. From there I trained with The International Yoga School. It's a good discipline to have. I'm very interested in alternative medicine so when I give up dancing I'd still want to be doing something using the body, I have to, I don't want to ever seize up.

The fundamental thing in a dancing career is to never accept 'no' as an answer – keep going! A lot of dancers are obsessed with working in London because it's the capital and they think if you're good then it's the place to work, which is not the case at all. You have got to be happy with what you are doing and what you want to do. I was always told 'stick at it, your time will come'. I don't have an ambition as such, but I have always had goals. You have to have goals to aim for and a standard to reach otherwise you just drift. Never become complacent; we are all unique and everyone who enters this profession has something to offer. Good luck!

Chapter Fourteen

Choreographers

Choreography is the composition of steps put together to create a dance. The choreographer is the person who creates these steps. Choreography is used for all kinds of jobs, not just dance shows, and a choreographer may be asked to work with backing singers or actors who have to 'move' in a production, for example. They are also at the core of vast productions such as ice-skating and gymnastics, and may even go as far as compiling moves for stunt artistes and stage fighters.

It is the choreographer's job to create original material for artists to perform. Before they begin a job they will have several meetings with their client to find out as much about the job as possible. The client may have a strong vision and want the chore-ographer to bring it to life, or he may ask him to paint the complete picture himself and rely on the imagination of the choreographer. Music is often the main inspiration, and once the music has been chosen a flood of ideas transpire and appropriate steps are invented. At other times a show or video may have a strong link with a certain subject or a theme on which the foundations of the steps are based, for example a jungle theme creates an image on its own, as does a futuristic number. There are dance steps which made their mark in history for each decade of the 20th century, and recreating these steps is great fun for a chore-ographer, as is costuming the routine. Anyone who has been to a 60s or 70s night will know what I mean. A choreographer has to be conscientious as their job involves a great deal of preparation. Before they turn up to a job they usually work through some ideas on their own so they are ready to teach the dancers their material.

The choreographer is often given a lot more to do than create a show. They may have to audition dancers, read through CVs and choose dancers, go shopping for suitable music, have meetings with musical directors, talk to the client, make sure costumes are suitable for their routines, talk through the dancers' contracts with any agents and finally prepare their material well enough to begin teaching the dancers on rehearsal day. The list goes on and once a production has commenced the choreographer's task changes direction to a kind of mother role. He is the one the dancers look to for reassurance and help with their problems or injuries. It is an exhausting job, mentally and physically. A choreographer will be concerned how his production looks, but at the same time be babysitting his team of dancers and smoothing over any ripples backstage. It can end up a management, wardrobe, directing and choreographing job all rolled into one! This is not always the case and with larger productions the choreographer is part of a team. They work alongside a director, producer, musical director and assistant choreographer – together they will come up with the finished product. This has the advantage of allowing choreographers to worry only about their own job, which is a lot less stressful, but it does mean that decisions have to be agreed by all parties and it doesn't allow as much freedom of choice.

Choreographers are looked up to in the dancing industry as they are often the link between a client and an agent, and that means work for dancers. A lot of choreographers teach as well and it is good for a dancer to build a rapport with choreographers during lessons or engagements. During a choreographer's career if they meet dancers they enjoy working with and if their production was successful, you can bet your life they will use the same dancers again at some point down the line. They often assign a head dancer or an assistant who can take over when the choreographer is away. For some jobs the choreographer is hired to choreograph the show and rehearse it, then their part is done. They may be asked back much later to do extra rehearsals or replace new dancers. From the point when the choreographer is happy that the show is ready and has seen the start of the run, they depart and leave their head dancer in charge. This is excellent training for a potential choreographer and she will have to make decisions and give instructions to the team to the extent of shuffling the choreographer's work about and replacing sections if dancers fall ill or things are not working as well as they should. She will do whatever she thinks suitable to keep the show up to standard.

To become a choreographer you must have the passion and skill to compile new and innovative dances, you need the ability to communicate with people and pull out the best possible performance from your dancers, you must have an eye for detail and not watch just one part of a performance but see it as a complete polished production, and you must have patience as good creations don't fall into place immediately. Be together and be creative and you have the qualities of a potential choreographer. Choreographers get paid considerably more than dancers as there is a lot more to their job. They may be paid an hourly or daily rate for their work or they may negotiate a total fee for the entire production. It varies with each job. Unlike dancers, once they have a few credits on their CV choreographers, particularly commercial choreographers, can put their fees up accordingly. Bear in mind that a choreographer just starting out may be paid nothing for their effort because they want a chance and can see an opening. They will approach a client or company and ask to choreograph just for the experience. Once a choreographer has worked he can begin to collect excerpts of video footage from each job and compile a showreel to produce to clients to get more work. Without this a choreographer may have to show his work to clients in other ways, perhaps asking dancer friends to dance one of his pieces in front of the client in a rehearsal studio or, as I mentioned, to work for no pay until he's proved himself. All this takes time and energy and if it is possible to provide a showreel then you can run off copies to give to your agent to tout about. A successful choreographer on the other hand can then let their reputation go before them and obtain work by recommendation only. If work starts to snowball then fees can shoot through the roof, because the choreographer's name is associated with a successful production or smash hit band.

Profile of choreographer Kevan Allen

Kevan Allen *is one of Britain's youngest, most successful choreographers specialising in the corporate entertainment industry. His credits include directing, styling and choreographing acclaimed shows for Wella International, Coca Cola, British Airways, Citroen, Rover and Woolworths. Theatre work includes The George Gershwin Gala at the London Palladium and the '97 UK tour of What A Feeling. He has choreographed commercials for KP Skips, Ariel Automatic and Wash & Go and staged productions for corporate and fashion industries, Benetton, The Gap, Levis Strauss and The Walt Disney Group.*

I trained at Arts Educational School for three years altogether, and before that I went to an amateur dance school called The Essex Dance Theatre. My sister's three years older than me and she's an actress. She had drama classes there and she took me along to get me out of my shell and I took to movement like a duck to water. I ended up doing more movement than drama and one day someone came down from Arts Educational, picked me out and offered me a place to train full-time with a grant. I could have gone to The Royal Ballet School when I was 12 but I didn't want to do ballet. I wanted to do more jazz stuff. I was very sensible, I waited until I was 16 and did my O Levels first! I think I always knew I wanted to be in the theatre, but as what, I don't know. I didn't ever want to be a choreographer – how I'm doing what I'm doing I don't really know, it's all a bit of a mystery!

When I was at college you had to have your Equity card to work, so I formed my own dance company called Beauxartz. It was just like a hobby. Me and a few friends would rehearse in the studios after college or in the holidays. I literally did everything – choreographed the numbers, designed the costumes, made the costumes, edited the music, did the bookings, the whole thing. There was eight of us in the group and it was like a sort of game. We were 16 and we didn't care – we had so much energy we just went for it! We did gigs to get our Equity. Our first one was back at The Essex Dance Theatre School where I trained. They would put on huge summer shows and book us as the top of the bill and give us a contract towards getting our cards. The Embassy Club was very good at the time. Libby Rose, Arlene Phillips and Hot Gossip were coming out, so Beauxartz kind of came out in the right vogue. Wherever Hot Gossip went we seemed to follow, they knew about us and we knew about them. We were sort of like them but a much more dancified, arty version. It was the right timing. Then I didn't care what I did – I had the most bizarre ideas and dreams and made everybody do it. Looking back it was outrageous! But at the time you don't realise what you're doing. Now I think 'My god, what were we wearing!' Lisa Jones says 'Oh I had a whip! I had a whip!' and now it seems really kinky, but at the time we thought nothing of it, it was just very 80s. We did lots of clubs and then somebody from a corporate company who were launching a new thing called 'Prism Robot' came to see one of our shows. They wanted a few pretty girls round it and they thought the idea of a self-contained group would be good. That became our first big show and we were in seventh heaven. We got paid about £600 total and we couldn't believe it, we were used to getting a tenner a night if we were lucky. We thought we'd really made it!

I was about to stop doing Beauxartz but it had built up such a reputation, there was such a buzz about it, everyone knew us including people like Arlene Phillips who was so supportive and was saying 'What this guy is doing is brilliant' and 'The group's fantastic'. She was very interested. So we thought we must have *something*! There was a new television series on Channel 4 called *ECT* which followed on after *The Tube* broke. It was a live heavy metal show which had never been done before and the director Keith McMillan wanted a self-contained dance group to appear on the show each week. He began scouting around and he said wherever he went people recommended Beauxartz. So he came down to some of our rehearsals at Pineapple and then offered us the job of the ten-week television series. He intended on using Anthony Van Last to choreograph it but when he saw us he said 'No, I'd like Kevan to do it'. That was my big break.

I choreographed and danced in Beauxartz but at the same time I was working elsewhere as a dancer. It was the big video boom of the 80s. My first job was with Olivia Newton John, then I did Tina Turner. One of the biggest jobs was the Duran Duran video 'Wild Boys'. I was actually the bald-headed wild boy, which was a brilliant thing to have done because it was such a turning point in the making of videos. It was also hell to do, five hours' make-up per day and feeling physically ill by the end of it because I was breathing in the fumes of the plastic coating of my make-up, and dancing long hours for two weeks, but I was working with some really influential people so I was in the right place at the right time.

I've never been pushy, which can go against me, but people just got to hear about what I was doing without me having to drop showreels on their laps. They used to say 'Oh Kevan, where are you next performing?' and they'd see my work and then ask me to choreograph for them. I was getting more and more choreographic stuff and it got to a point where I was getting lots of freelance work as a choreographer. Whenever I was choreographing I always used to incorporate the dancers from the group, but it became increasingly difficult because every job is different and directors sometimes asked for six blonde girls – well, I didn't have six blonde girls in the group and it became harder to be loyal to all of them, so I stopped the group at the peak of its success. It had gone brilliantly well and rather than flog a dead horse I thought I'd stop on a high. Also I was tired. It had been going for eight years and I'd been doing everything, nobody else in the group did anything other than support me. It was very flattering that they never queried me. They never said 'I'm not wearing that, I'm not doing that'. They just did and wore whatever I said. So I stopped the group and just carried on with the choreographing which snowballed!

I've always managed myself. When I left college I got my first audition dancing on the Olivia Newton John job. We were rehearsing at Pineapple studios and David Paton from Pineapple agency saw me and said 'I'd like that boy to come and see me' and he took me on. And that was my first agent. Then as all dancers do, you join all of the agencies. To be honest Pineapple were the main ones at the time, they were helping the group and helping me as a choreographer.

I look very young for my age, which has also gone against me, and up until the last five years clients would see someone older and assume they had a lot more experience than me, but now my name goes before me. As I say, I'm not very pushy and I believe hard work speaks for itself. If you are really good at what you do you don't have to keep bragging about it. You just turn up, do your job, and be professional. Also you have to enjoy what you're doing. The minute I hate doing what I'm doing I'm not going to do it any more. I won't have a rehearsal if there's a bad atmosphere or work with people that I think are bad apples and have an attitude. Personality is just as important as dancing ability. I like teamwork and I like to have a laugh; the minute it gets stressful I'm not going to do it and I think that does pay off.

Working as a dancer has changed tremendously and I don't think for the better. When I came out of college you had to *be* hot, you had to be able to do everything: triple pirouettes, jetés, be a bendy machine, break your back – pull anything out the bag they wanted! Nowadays all they want to do is be pop stars. It's all about image. Every dancer has the best outfits but no technique. They don't think it's important so they don't keep it up. If you're going to be driven around in limousines and go and dance on *Top Of The Pops* – what a life! But where is the sweat, the grit and the kicking legs! I used to come home with that brilliant aching feeling of

'My god, I've used every single muscle in my body' and it was great. I blame a mixture of things within the industry, especially corporate, commercial and pop work. They don't know a good choreographer from a bad choreographer because they don't understand dance. They see that dancers look groovy and can dance, but they are not pushing for anything better. There's certain people that manipulate the whole of the pop industry at the moment and it's sad really, because every new artiste that comes out looks exactly the same, the dancers do exactly the same thing, choreography is exactly the same . . . They haven't got the knowledge or expansion to do anything different. But the record companies think 'Oh well, they've been number one for two weeks, we'll get their choreographer in'. Therefore all the work that is going around is the same. Consequently the students at college who are training in contemporary, ballet, are thinking 'I don't want to do this, I want to do *that* style, so I don't really need to do all this technical stuff' and they don't concentrate on it. Therefore the standard is dropping. It's like a big vicious circle. That's why I'm adamant – when a dancer works for me they are going to kick arse and are going to sweat and ache. It's a love/hate thing. I can see they are suffering when I set penchée into split, but they always say 'It's so nice to dance again, we love it!'.

There are many more younger choreographers now. I mean, I'm young but some of them are still in their 20s! When I was dancing there were choreographers like George May, Jeff Richer, Alan Harding, Anthony Van Last, Arlene, all older and much more experienced. They were all doing the jobs that I'm now doing and they have moved on and become directors or are working in America. So I have filled that whole gap and cornered virtually all of the corporate market as number one choreographer, which is brilliant. You do need experience before you can say you are a choreographer. I don't think choreography is just about putting steps together. Steps are the last part of choreography, you have to create the whole atmosphere, the ideas, the music, the ambience, the feel, the lights. When you've got all those pieces you then fuse it together with the steps, which makes it all come to life. It's the staging, that's what makes the whole thing work. Choreography is so much more, people don't comprehend what it actually entails.

I'm very critical and there's not many choreographers working today that I have much respect for. I like Sir Kenneth McMillan from The Royal Ballet, I like everything he's done. He does incredible partner work, I love the way he makes dancer's bodies entwine. Susan Stroman is really, really talented, she's done *Oklahoma* and *Crazy for You*.

When I get a job the ideas vary. Sometimes a client will ask me to fill an hour with whatever I want to do, or they will give me a few ingredients, for example a motif of the colour blue and a trademark of an eagle, then I create something with that and make it work. I prefer to do my own thing. My main love is music because it inspires me to choreograph. I love absolutely everything from classical to heavy metal to funk and R&B, you name it! My choreography is very diverse, people find it hard to pigeonhole me. I do everything from ballet, to contemporary, to jazz, to tap, to funky, I've done everything! Why should I do one thing? I've just had a meeting in LA with an agency that represent 50 choreographers who all have their own niche and they just do that one style of choreography. They looked at my showreel and of course they couldn't fit me into any one niche because there is every style on there.

I did a lot of Kylie's stuff and I've done the Bucketheads and Bryan Ferry. I tend to do the ones that are slightly more avant garde. If they want something really different, then they get me in. I do a lot for The Walt Disney Special Events Group worldwide, staging productions for corporate events. During Spring '97 I was in Dubai launching The Disney Channel in The Middle East. Disney is fantastic and very clued-up, but at the same time very squeaky clean. So they asked me in about two years ago to update and twist it slightly and make it more acceptable to the European market, so I'm trying to slowly make it a bit more funky. The audiences are responding – most of the shows I do in Europe get standing ovations. I don't work for them full-time as they wanted someone who does other things as well. It's nice, I just come in and do my bit. I grew up with Disney, I love it!

I sometimes miss dancing. I recently did some classes on Broadway in New York and nobody knew me and I really enjoyed it, but I prefer to stay on the creative side. I'm very close to the dancers I work with and they always say it's very bizarre to have a choreographer who comes in and hasn't thought about the steps until the rehearsal starts at 10 o' clock. When the tape goes on I make it up on the spot, and then get the dancers to try it. I know what I want. I do everything by myself, I don't have any input from anybody else. That way it's so refreshing for the dancers because two days later I know exactly what I set and we can deal with it there and then, instead of people saying 'the counts have changed'. I more or less try and use the same pool of dancers I know I can rely on and then I introduce new dancers within them. That way they get carried along with the professionalism of the others. Now I find new dancers by recommendation. I haven't auditioned for years, I don't have the time, and I hate the whole audition process. Because of the level I've reached now, I'm asked to create a show on the back of what they've seen me do before, so they expect a certain standard and to reach that I expect a high standard from my dancers, and they are very few and far between. I can tell you exactly who they are in London and exactly who they are in New York. I'd say there's about 30–40 in London who cut it. They have all the technique, are punctual, professional, a joy to work with and they 'pull it off'. I don't have to worry. Out of 40 dancers I'd say about 15 are male. Sophie from 'Sophie's People' represents me and I get to hear about new dancers from her. I may see their details and keep them on file and if something comes up they are maybe right for, I'll meet them. I'm a great one for personality, I can normally tell straight away if we are going to click.

I did some guest teaching at Pineapple but I don't really enjoy it, it's not creative. I'm terrible – I like to work with people who are brilliant and I get frustrated when I can't do something with dancers that I want to.

I've worked bloody hard to get where I am and I've always been very confident. Every audition I've done I've thought 'I can do this' and I have nearly always been the best guy there. It really annoys me when people say it's easier for a boy to work as a dancer because the ratio is the same as for the girls. There are less boy dancers, but there are less jobs. I do pick and choose the work I do now, which is a nice position to be in. The last two years has been full-on, non-stop, I really haven't had any time off and I'm booked up to God knows when. In between the rehearsals I have numerous meetings because I design the costumes, plot the lighting, I do absolutely everything. I work quite a lot with stylist Carol Hoffman; she used to be a dancer and we work closely together. She knows what I like and my style and she also knows what is suitable to dance in. Basically I can work non-stop now until the day I die doing what I'm doing if I want to and it's great work, but I actually want to be a bit more than that. I'd like to have a 'name' like Fosse has a name. I would love to do a West End or Broadway show. I have done a lot of one-off specials and charity shows like Gershwin and Sondheim, but again it's a closed circuit. I'm classed as very avant garde and commercial and young. If I'd had a background of just West End they might trust me. It's funny because when they've seen my Gershwin shows in the past they've said 'My God, you are incredible, why don't you do a West End show?'

I will always have a passion for singing but I've knocked that on the head because of the way the music industry works. It is something I really would like to do but I never realised it, so there you go. I am in the process of forming my own dance company and that is really what I'd like to do next. Not a dance company that's been around before though. It will be pushed in a very positive, publicised and commercial way. It's got to have the right vibe and be purely dance with a mixture of styles and hot dancers who could go into The Royal Ballet but have chosen Kevan's company instead! So at that level it has the respect of the critics but is set towards the people who love music and dance and pop concerts.

Profile of choreographer Priscilla Samuels

Priscilla Samuels *is one of Britain's leading choreographers in the music industry and has worked with The Spice Girls.*

I was a dancer before I became a choreographer. I didn't train at any of the flash colleges. I took up dancing as a hobby. My mum and dad sent me to a dancing school called The Wheatly School of Dancing in Catford to do ballet, tap and stage three evenings a week at the age of eight on the International Dance Teachers Association (IDTA) syllabus.

I wasn't really inclined to become a dancer and my mum and dad wanted me to get an education first, so after my O Levels I went to college to do a BTec National Diploma. At 17 I was working 9–5 in Channel 4 accounts department then for a fashion company. I hadn't really found my way yet career wise. I was still doing my dance classes at the school and performing in their end-of-year shows. I got into a bit of video work as an extra, freestyling on them. I started to buy *The Stage* and go along to a few auditions to see what it was all about. My mum and dad said to me 'If you really want to be a dancer then go for it!', so I got hold of all the agencies and auditioned for them. I just persisted. I got told no thank you for certain jobs and I thought 'right, I'm going to put all my heart into this!'

My lucky break was dancing for Cathy Dennis who was big at that time. I was booked to do another job and it fell through, but fortunately the record company still wanted to see me and I ended up getting the job for Cathy just as she was about to tour The States. So at 18 I was a full-time dancer touring America. I worked for her for about four years. My first choreographic job was for Cathy Denis too. It came about by me saying 'I'd like to be a choreographer eventually', and they gave me the chance. After that I didn't think 'right, now I'm going to be a choreographer'. I carried on dancing. I still wanted to dance for other people, I was auditioning for work and doing backing dancing jobs. I eased into choreography. I think if I'd stopped dancing then I would have lost something that has helped me get where I am now. I've always remained within the music industry. I went on to do Apache Indian, Beloved, Chaka Demus & Pliers, Shaggy . . . Once I got in with a record company and got on with the right people, they would find out I had choreographed Cathy Dennis and Apache Indian and then offer me one of the acts on their label, it's all about contacts.

I was a regular dancer on *Top Of The Pops*. In fact after about 18 months of regularly dancing on the show, they put my name on a dressing room door because I was booked so often! I used to keep changing my hair style to make myself look different. Once I was phoned and they said 'We need dancers for Shaggy real quick!' I made something up on the spot when I got there for 'Oh Carolina' and then it went to number one in the charts and stayed there for three weeks. Whenever an act used to turn up for *Top Of The Pops* without dancers I used to get the last-minute call, usually on the filming day and they'd say 'Can you come down and bring some dancers with you?' It was a different system to what it is now.

I can honestly say with my hand on my heart I have never touted for any work. I've never even had a showreel. I don't to this day because I don't like to change some things. I can produce a CV if I'm asked, but generally I work by word of mouth. If you know me, then you know my work and if you don't, you don't. Being an active dancer and a choreographer, people were seeing me perform at the same time as seeing my choreography and word just got around. Once you've got a job you have to put your all into it and do a good job, because if it goes well it will pay off. Now people phone me up and they know they will have to pay a certain fee if they come to me. I have to stand up for myself and I won't settle for less because I know I'm worth it. There was a time when I'd accept everything, but gradually with experience you have to get out of that and set your standards high. I'm not going above myself because even now if the music is right and I like the job, I will do it whatever the budget or even for nothing if my heart's in it. It's about job satisfaction. I pick and choose what I choreograph. If something's not my style I don't do it. I think too many choreographers do everything and don't master in a style. If you choreograph a certain style you should specialise in it, to make the whole industry over here better. Everyone always says America have got this and that, well I've been there and done that. I've auditioned dancers in the States often enough and I do believe we have got all that we need here in the UK, but it should be up to the choreographer to teach the dancer his or her style. It's up to them to nurture it and bring it out. My imagination can go wild and I am creative. I know I was put on to the earth to do what I'm doing now. The blessing is I love what I do and that drives me to seek and learn more. I never think 'that's it', there is always something else to move on to and I'm happy!

If you work with an artiste you have to spend the first half hour showing off so they get a taste of what you can do, especially when you're a girl choreographing for a boy band. They don't think you can work them so sometimes you have to prove a point and that way they sit back and think 'Ok, we'll listen to you, you obviously mean business'. There aren't that many active choreographers (still dancing) and I can choreograph boys as well as I do girls and still demonstrate what it should look like. Artistes should be out there doing what they do best, whereas dancers are trained so I usually give them more moves to deal with because they are trained to cope with it.

Choreographing for The Spice Girls came about when I was approached by their ex-management to come in and coach them before their major deal. I had these five girls in the studio and they all had this different look: Emma had the wedged pink shoes on,

Geri had the Vivienne Westwood boots on, Victoria was feminine and controlled, Mel B flamboyant and Mel C had on an Adidas tracksuit, and that night I went home and my friends still remind me of what I said. I said 'These girls are going to be absolutely massive' because their energy was so far-fetched and the act was totally different. They followed on after Take That when the music industry was male-dominated. The marketing was extremely clever, their songs were energetic and pop and it was the right niche at the right time. Timing is very important, everything in the music industry is down to timing and The Spice Girls couldn't have been more correct. In the beginning they really wanted to do all their choreography themselves. Two of them had trained as dancers and they didn't necessarily need a choreographer. You often get that if an artiste can dance. But lucky for me I gained the girls' respect pretty early on because they said 'We know you, we've seen you dance on TV . . .' So they knew I could do whatever I was going to tell them to do and I gained their trust straight away.

I started off by coaching them on bringing out their individual personalities and working out little routines. After the number one record 'Wannabe', their profile rocketed and they did become massive. I choreographed everything they've done from the start to SpiceWorld Tour '98. To find the Spice Boy dancers took me over two months. The girls said whatever it takes we'll sort it out, so I took my time. We were looking for guys to match the girls; and I knew what I wanted. From working round Europe I'd crossed paths with dancers who were talented. It's also about a look; you watch an American video and see how amazing the guys look and how they move. The grooming of a male dancer has to be so correct. You can't just put the latest trainers on or cut your hair a certain way as it will come across as false, it's not about that. You can come in with a pair of boots on and if you are groomed and carry yourself with confidence people accept that you are who you are. I wanted all the guys to be different races, different colours, like The United Colours of Benetton! I scouted all the dancers I'd seen in the past and asked some of them to send over video tapes of them dancing and I got together the final seven guys. We rehearsed in Dublin for five weeks and the dancers only had about three and a half weeks to learn the complete show. For The SpiceWorld Tour the girls put their trust in me and I was given the title of choreographer and show producer, so needless to say I was busy from then on! I treat choreographing The Spice Girls like any other job. I don't think I've had my best job to date yet. My dream would be to have five dancers that move like Janet Jackson and a huge budget to create something wild. I'd take my time to cruise Europe to find the best diva dancers, male and female.

I think more attention should be paid to dancers and the investment in dancers, for example in the editing of videos. If we look at the dancers in American videos, we actually get to see the choreography and the talent. Janet Jackson videos are based around dance. Over here the editing is so chopped and sharp, you barely see an arm or a leg and it's not making the most of our dancers. They should raise their profile and realise what they can contribute to a production. Maybe we need more directors with a dance background – maybe I should become a director!

All types of dance deserve respect. If you can spin on your head I'll give you respect for doing it, if you twinkle on your toes I'll give you respect for doing that as well. No dancer's style is better than another, whoever they are. They all studied their technique and they deserve recognition for that. If someone recognises me as a dancer I take it as such a compliment, I can't ask for more than that.

I think some dancers are involved in the music industry for the wrong reasons. I remember when backing an artiste wasn't a very profitable or cool thing to do; now, because of the status of the music industry you've got every dancer from trade shows and musicals wanting to work with pop stars, doing the videos and tours and even trying to be the actual bands! The danger is that it's not about the love of it any more, it's about the hierarchy and the fame which is all wrong. They're not stars, they don't twinkle above my house at night and dancers shouldn't rise to them.

I have a company Massive Creation Ltd which is basically a team of choreographers who work with me. I call myself the executive choreographer because clients will call up and ask for me, but I couldn't spread myself around that much, so the best way round that was to start a company with choreographers who have a strong style. Also, if work comes in that's not up my alley then I'll pass it on to the right choreographer to do it. I always oversee the jobs and make sure the client is getting the style he or she wants. Sometimes we share jobs because we need each other's ideas. It's nice to have another choreographer in the room saying

'Why don't we try it this way?' It's teamwork which is what it is all about. I am very business minded and I was lucky to learn marketing, word processing and management skills at college before I danced, and I thank my mum and dad for guiding my career so that I covered all that, however desperate I was to dance. Because a dancer's career isn't that long you have to seek something else to do, know what to move on to. I wanted to dance, then I moved on to choreography and it's been a whole learning process really for what I intend on doing next. I want to go into management, manage music acts. I've also thought about directing.

I like to have my finger in lots of pies and I get lots of encouragement from people about going into management. People have said I'm a woman who has a certain amount of power and can stand up for myself. I can deal with men in the industry just as easily as I can deal with women. Because I handle all my work and all my choreographer's work I think that's half the grooming I need for management. I deal with all kinds of problems. There are very few female managers and I think I've got the balls to do it. I've always managed myself, apart from in the very beginning when I got dancing work through the agencies. I have had agents who have wanted to sign me up for sole representation, but I have almost always got my own choreographic work, and I have management skills, so I prefer to do it myself, I enjoy the challenge of it. Music and dancing is my first love. I would eventually like to manage an artiste or a couple of acts, manage the stylist, the choreographer/s, dancers, have a studio to work in and have everything in-house with a perfect professional team all on the same wavelength.

Part Three
The Business Of Being A Dancer

Dancing has become a large part of your life – maybe you began dancing from an early age, or worked professionally as a child, appearing in a local pantomime or a TV commercial, or perhaps you entered a full-time college for performing arts. Whatever kind of training you have obtained so far, it will eventually take you to the gates of 'the professional industry', the moment when you have to get work! You have become a business and have to earn money to live, pay rent, run a car and pay for a phone; you have to keep files, log your income and expenditure and be responsible for your own tax affairs.

This section is designed to help you understand the business side of a dancing career. It will help motivate you into finding work, tell you how to go about looking after yourself, and give you advice to follow and examples to adapt to your own ideas for running your business.

Chapter Fifteen

Getting Organised

Organisation and motivation

It's time to put all the advice you've received into action. All the training, good looks and luck in the world won't mean a thing unless you are an organised motivated dancer. A Formula One racing car is full of power, but it still needs a driver. A dancer who set out with dreams and ambition will undoubtedly have the necessary drive to succeed in the beginning; the danger comes when you have had so many knock-backs and you have given your best, yet you have no job to show for it. Once you have accepted that rejection is part of the industry and have learned to deal with it you are halfway there. Keep your desire to dance and reach out for your ambitions – if you persevere for long enough it will pay off.

As a dancer, there is so much to discover, so many types of dancing jobs, people to meet, places to visit. A dancer's career can cover so much ground, but you must keep reminding yourself of what you want to achieve. You have to learn to be consistent and accept that dancing work is erratic. A dancer has to condition herself to cope with many career moves, some good, some not so good, and find a happy medium where she can deal with the decisions she's made and whatever waits around the next corner. If the going is good and you have five wonderful consecutive jobs, it is easy to become accustomed to 'the good life' – nice work, lots of attention, good pay, great costumes, wild choreography, huge response from the audience and then . . . nothing. This may sound extreme, but sometimes you will fall on stony ground after a job and it may make you feel low. These are the times a dancer needs to dig deep and get motivated again. Don't give up! Your career is going to be full of highs and lows, so ride with it and hold on to the high times to carry you through the low times. There will be a new challenge along soon!

Making use of time

A successful dancer is one who can sit back for a period without any work and make use of the time. Make some intelligent decisions, after all you don't know when your next job will be, it may be tomorrow or it may be in a month's time. Think about it logically – there are so many other parts to your career that you need to catch up on and explore while you're not being booked out for work.

Firstly, enjoy a rest. You never know how many more calm times in your life you will experience, so cherish every minute. You can take your time to do all the things you dreamt of when you were away on tour or training at college; go shopping, pamper yourself in a long bath, appreciate some good food or listen to some inspiring music. Once you feel rested, if you're still not ready to spring back into action, take time to catch up on your accounts, collect all your receipts from your jacket pockets and sort them into months. This will save you money in the long run as you will claim expenses from your tax and save on your accountancy bill too. Make use of this precious time to update your CV or write to a new agent. If you are looking rested it may be the perfect opportunity to have new pictures taken. There is something you can do every day that will enhance your career, something as simple as a phone call to an agent or choreographer to remind them you are available for future work. If you're not in the mood to speak to them, then make it less formal and have a chat with a few dancing pals and catch up on the gossip, they may know about some forthcoming work that you haven't heard about, especially if you've been away.

Making use of time takes practice. It's easy for an unemployed dancer to sit indoors watching unhealthy amounts of daytime television and thinking there will be something around the corner. Often there is, but you need to instigate it. If you find it hard doing these things alone, try doing it with another dancer in the same position. You could drag yourselves to a class together, then sit and discuss your aches and pains over a cup of coffee. Talk to your parents. Parents love to help and if you live away from home go back and visit them for a few days. This is often a great way to put things back in perspective. Late night chats with your mum or dad about you, your life and politics can help with your career direction or any decisions you need to make.

Don't ever get bogged down with too much free time and nothing to fill it. Have a rest, then get busy organising your life again and things will gradually fall into place.

Top tips from the professionals

Get a good understanding of the career and gather advice from people who have done it. It's a fabulous life to lead – it's very exciting but have a back-up plan for financial reasons. Sometimes life as a dancer is limited, but if there's something you really want to do you've just got to do it!   Harri

Don't dance for free, always get paid for your art and don't wear leg warmers! Get as much advice from other people as possible. Don't be afraid to ask.   Alicia

Be aware of the ups and downs; if you have a good month you will always get a bad month too. Sometimes it's brilliant and other times it's not. If you want to sing and dance then definitely have some singing lessons to learn how to breathe properly. Just get out there and try it out, either with a band or in a club, anything to build your confidence.   Helen

Always put some money by. Even if you do a great job for a couple of thousand pounds, never go mad and spend it all. Save some for tax purposes and for the times when you may not work because you just never know with commercial dancing; when you think the going is good things can change. There's not many dancing jobs and trends come and go so fast you may be working constantly one month then no-one wants you the next, and all because your hair style is no longer hip, it's as quick as that!
                                                    Michelle

You need to be persistent because there are so many rejections and really so much of it has to do with your look and not your talent. You can't take it personally, you just have to keep on going and pushing, pushing. It may take years, but it'll happen as long as you are driven.   Lisa S

Get great pictures of what you actually look like. So many dancers look wonderful in the flesh, but you see their photos and they're far too glamorous – hair slicked back, too much make-up etc. It's not necessary to look so modelly; natural photos will get you more work. Build your career at a pace you can handle and make sure you know what you are doing, learn your craft. It's no good blagging your way through as a dancer, there are far too many of them out there!

Lyndon

Go to Pineapple to pick up the latest dance style, find out about auditions and make friends with people already working in the industry. Just by watching the dancers there, you will learn what to wear and how to wear make-up etc.

Sam

Never ever forget that there is a life outside dancing, otherwise you will get very disillusioned very quickly. You aren't expected to eat, sleep and breath dancing, but it doesn't always seem that way – it's actually good for you to take a step outside of it all and do something detached from the industry to help you put life back into perspective.

Charlotte

Get some photos! A nice head shot and a good body shot, then go and visit all the agencies. Keep ringing them and go to auditions, but it takes a good 12 months to get going and establish yourself. If you don't get chosen, it's not because you're not good enough, it's because your hair's the wrong colour, so to keep on going you must have drive and ambition. Remember who you are, don't get too wrapped up in it all. Be quietly confident. If you want it that badly then you can get there! Don't take all the rejections to heart.

Lisa J

Make sure you get some training, then start doing auditions for experience. See what's out there and see what you've got to aim for – the look as well as the style and standard of dancing. For musicals make sure you get the right song that works for you.

David

Have a goal in life, you've got to have determination! You are going to go to endless auditions. I didn't get my first job until six months after I'd been turned down at every single audition I'd been to, and that's a long time. So do not be put off by rejection. I think it's essential to be 100 per cent reliable and to have as many special skills as possible, and to me the most important thing is to look good. When I auditioned for the Beat Girls, they only wanted one girl and there were about 170 girls there and I know I got it for two reasons – I wore the brightest top I could find, it was actually fluorescent orange!, and I let my personality come through. The competition out there is so fierce that you have *got to* stand out! Dee Dee

Don't shun your college training, keep it up. One day someone will say – double pirouette, drop into box splits! Be nice to everyone. All over the world dancers know each other – it's a close circuit, so don't back stab anyone otherwise I won't work with you! Kevan

Know your own identity; make sure you *have* an identity. You can tell a new dancer by what they are wearing. Whether it's your hair colour or your clothes, you have to carry it with confidence. If it's hip to wear then make sure your dancing lives up to the expectation of your image. Don't be a fake, don't dress up like a pop star and pretend to be something you're not. Image is so important. Dancers are artistes and should think that way in their grooming and in their mind. You have to love it, if you don't love it, don't do it! Priscilla

Chapter Sixteen

Getting Down to Business

Confirmed for the job

You researched the job, you auditioned for the job, and you've got the job – congratulations! Now it is essential that you prepare for the job.

Showing your professionalism and being conscientious about the work you've been offered will only be to your advantage and possibly lead to new contacts or even more work. You may have been confirmed for the job via your agent who will organise all the necessary contracts and relevant details for your rehearsals and performance. He will negotiate your payment and collect it by return of invoice after the job, then charge you a commission for his efforts (see 'Agents'). If you got the job by yourself (via an open audition or personal contact), then it is down to you to organise everything. You must take steps to make sure you have all the details for the job.

- the job description
- the company name and address
- the client's name and address
- date of performance/s
- time of performance/s
- address for the job
- date of rehearsals
- time of rehearsals
- contract or letter offering you the job (always get some kind of confirmation; this is essential if there is a problem with you getting paid)
- the fee and type of payment
- invoice details if necessary (maybe a different address to send it to)
- wardrobe/costume fittings or details of clothes and accessories to bring
- notes to remember (choreographer's name on arrival or the other dancers' phone numbers etc.).

Most companies are organised enough to have the majority of the details listed ready for you in a letter at the confirmation of the job. Prior to the audition or casting, the dancers will hand in their CV with their contact address on it, or fill in a separate sheet given to them on arrival. The chosen few will be telephoned later that day or the next day, directly or via their agent to confirm their availability and interest in the job, then a letter or contract will follow afterwards. Some clients may not be so efficient, especially if the job has evolved via a friend of a friend. If you have scribbled details down at the audition or over the phone on a scrap of paper, you need to refer to your check list and then make sense of your notes by copying them down clearly into your diary. Keep any paperwork safe, you will need it later on to get paid for your work and for your tax return.

Once your job is secure you can be happy at the thought that you are presently a 'working' dancer. Now you must concentrate on showing your talent and reliability. Remember you have to maintain your good reputation and 'shine' for the clients without trying too hard. It is possible for young dancers to appear too keen and become quite irritating. On the day of the rehearsal make sure you have everything you need. The choreographer may ask you to bring along knee pads for floor work or the client may ask for passport details for contracts abroad. Plan ahead and pack anything relevant to the job you're dancing on. Always allow extra time for travelling on the first day of rehearsals as turning up late on day one is not a good start. Have contact numbers at the ready in case of unavoidable hold-ups on your journey. When you arrive at the job, check in with your contact name or spot the nearest person carrying a clipboard – they usually know what's going on. Make yourself known to someone, don't sit down in a corner assuming they know you've arrived. It won't be long before you are chatting away to other dancers, talking about the job you've been booked for and the previous audition day. This is exactly what you should do – be warm and friendly towards your fellow dancers, after all you will be expected to perform together as a team. However, remember to respect your choreographers and directors – they are trying to concentrate and create a production so save the noisy gossip for tea breaks. There may be long periods of hanging around, particularly on film sets, so try to be patient and polite no matter how bad your costume is. Avoid throwing a tantrum; you will only regret it later and not enjoy the job.

Laugh it off, things change all the time in rehearsals – one minute you may be cut from a number or asked to wear the green fluffy dragonfly costume, and the next you could be the central focus of the routine. So don't judge anyone too soon, keep your cool and enjoy yourself.

It is a good idea to keep a note of the time you arrived at your job and the time you finished. Depending on what has been negotiated and the type of dancing job, you may need to claim overtime payment for longer hours, or possibly reclaim expenses for getting home late – every job is different so always check what's included at the time of the initial booking. After the job tell your agent your total hours or include them on your own invoice along with photocopies of travel receipts and expenses to be reimbursed (don't send the originals, it's amazing how many get accidentally mislaid or lost by the recipient!).

Advice on contracts

There is only one way you can be certain the contract you have been given is legitimate, and that is to seek independent legal advice. It would be most inappropriate to see a lawyer for each one-day engagement you get, however. If you have an agent or the work came via one you will be in a better position, but there is still no guarantee you will be treated right and receive full payment. Nine out of ten jobs run without any hitches, and although many companies take weeks to pay up, they do pay. If you intend on taking very short and varied contracts throughout your career, then it is to be expected that occasionally one will end in sour grapes and refusal to pay for whatever reason. If this does happen, you must fight on and try and retrieve monies for work you have done. Always try and get documentation or written confirmation of a job, no matter how last minute. A fax will do, it is evidence and will put you in a stronger position should you need to visit a lawyer or small claims court. It sounds terribly callous, but it is only a reminder to be aware. There are a few sharks out there who want dancers for nothing and are full of false promises and fake contracts. Don't be 'a softy', don't be taken for granted, get written documentation to cover yourself and seek advice where necessary. Never walk into a dancing contract with your eyes shut, particularly when it involves leaving the country.

If you are considering a long contract or you want to get advice on the contract you've been given, contact The British Equity Association (see 'Listings'). They offer free legal advice to their members and if you are a non-member you can still telephone them and ask what they know about the company offering you work. You may find they have been black-listed. The safest contracts to sign are Equity contracts, negotiated and issued by themselves, or 'Equity approved' contracts, which means Equity have looked over them and approve of the terms. If something was to go wrong during either of these contracts then Equity would be in a position to sort out the problems on your behalf (providing you are a member).

Look out for the following points on a dancing contract:

- Dates: check the dates printed are correct.
- Rehearsal pay: check you will be paid for rehearsals.
- Fees: make sure all monies you expect to receive for rehearsals and performances are printed on your contract.
- Royalties: if it is a TV or film contract, contact Equity to make sure you get monies due for reruns or video sales worldwide. Royalties all add up.
- Accommodation: find out the type of accommodation – is it 3-4-, 5-star or a hostel? Get a full address and phone up to find out more; you will be miserable if your living accommodation isn't up to scratch.
- Travel: check travel is door to door, not just air flights. Get full details of inoculations needed for a country and the currency. Find out who you will be travelling with and how long you expect to stay on the road. Make sure you will be safe and comfortable and that details are in your contract.
- Food: bed and breakfast still leaves you two meals a day to find and pay for. If you are not going to have meals provided for you, try and get subsistence or per diems money to cover meals. This is only provided on contracts outside your home city.

Remember all these points – if they have been offered verbally at the audition, find out exactly what is included and ask for it to be put into your confirmation letter or contract.

Equity

The British Actors' Equity Association is a trade union representing performers across the entire spectrum of arts and entertainment. This includes dancers and all types of dancing contracts. Equity have established a wide range of collective agreements and standard contracts across the industry, and an Equity card is a symbol of professionalism throughout the entertainment business. Equity's motto is 'performing for you'. At some point in a dancer's career it is worth becoming a member. There are certain professional engagements such as some West End musicals that will only employ Equity members. Although Equity welcomes anyone who is working professionally in their recognised fields as a member, there are certain goals you must reach before they allow you in. You need to provide evidence of working as a professional performer in any of the following fields, usually in the form of a document or contract.

Theatre

You are required to have worked as a dancer in any form of theatre, engaged on the appropriate contract.

Opera and ballet

You are required to have worked as a dancer with a ballet or dance company on the appropriate contract.

Singers

You are required to have worked as a concert, session or pop singer – send evidence of one professional engagement.

Variety

You are required to have worked as a dancer who usually undertakes short-term engagements or gigs – send contractual evidence of no less than four of these within the same 12 months, plus one forthcoming engagement.

Television, film, commercials

You are required to have worked as a dancer engaged on the appropriate contract.

Working overseas

If you have worked professionally overseas you should provide proof of your employment, together with details, if any, of membership to a relevant union in the country concerned.

Other categories

As a student on a full-time performing arts course of more than one year, you can obtain student membership at a greatly reduced fee. If you are a student on an accredited dance course you will be eligible for Equity membership on graduation. If you are between 14 and 16 years of age and working for at least half the relevant adult rate, you can become an Equity youth member.

Equity cover many other areas of the entertainment industry and their policy applies to UK and EU citizens, or to citizens of other countries who have been granted permission to work in the UK as artists. Having Equity membership gives you access to essential advice throughout your career and helps you with career decisions by looking over contracts you have been offered or vetting a company for you. Some of the categories Equity cover include:

Pay and conditions

They negotiate minimum terms and conditions in all areas of the entertainment industry.

Help and advice

They can offer help with a range of services throughout your career. Their staff have specialist knowledge on terms of engagements and conditions of contracts etc.

Legal advice

They provide free legal advice on disputes over professional engagements, including personal injury claims.

Welfare advice

They provide free advice on National Insurance, taxation, benefits, pensions and welfare issues.

Royalties and residuals

They distribute royalties and residuals to members for TV and film reruns, video sales and recordings.

Registers

A large number of specialist registers are compiled by Equity and made available to casting directors and employers.

Campaigns

They campaign vigorously on behalf of their members on a wide range of issues.

Your professional name

They register your choice of professional name when you join, as long as it is not in use by another member.

Insurance

Public liability up to £2 million, backstage cover and accidental insurance are available free to all our members.

For full details on joining Equity contact your nearest regional office (see 'Listings').

Chapter Seventeen

Thinking about the Money!

Getting paid

After all that hard dancing work you still have to pay the bills! Getting paid as a dancer can be quite erratic. If you dance free-lance and do a number of different jobs over a short period of time, you will find payment for each job is different. Generally, getting paid for commercial jobs can take some time and you may not see your money for up to three months. This is because there is a chain of people involved and the finance has to pass through each source before it reaches you. For example, before you finally see your money from a day's booking dancing on a video shoot, it has to go through the following process:

(1) The record company provide a budget and pay a video company to organise a video shoot.
(2) The video company pay the artiste management company, who then pay a dance agency, who will pay you for dancing on the video. That's four accounting departments that your payment has to pass through before it reaches your hands, and each of those departments may take up to 28 days to pay an invoice. Try explaining all that to your landlord!

Other jobs are different and may just involve you and the client, narrowing the waiting time down immensely. And then there are the cash jobs. It is not unusual for a dancer to be paid in cash on the day of the job. But if there is no agent involved, always make sure you receive written confirmation prior to the booking, mentioning your fee for dancing, or alternatively insist you get paid *before* you dance. Failure to do this may mean it won't be long before you experience dancing for free! The secret in managing your money well is predicting when you will receive payments and making the money you have got last until then. Incoming payments that overlap may give you spare pennies to treat yourself!

How much you get paid will vary from job to job. Some

contracts are based on the Equity minimum (the amount Equity recommend as the lowest, most suitable fee for the job) – many companies pay just above this. If you are charging the client (as a freelance dancer this is inevitable), don't undersell yourself. If you are caught on the spot and asked to quote your fee without having time to think, ask for as many details of the job as possible. Find out the hours you will have to do and how involved the dancing will be. Then tell the client you will get back to him with your availability and fees.

Dancing is a specialised skill and it is difficult to relate it to a basic hourly wage. Just make sure you charge enough. If the client baulks at your quote you can always come down on the price, but you can't go up! As time goes on you will know what a job is worth to you and the current going rate for a day's dancing.

As you become established as a professional dancer, you will find your own suitable way of creating a consistent income. Some dancers have part-time work (dancing or otherwise) that provides a regular income to cover their outgoings. Other dancers use money from the big, well-paid jobs and put some by in reserve to live off while waiting for other payments to arrive. You will eventually work out who are the slow payers and bear this in mind on acceptance of the work. If your work is via your agent, ask them the terms of payment so you can at least plan ahead. If you prefer a weekly wage, then long contracts are for you. Musicals, showbars, cruises and theatre shows all issue contracts and specify the payment terms. You may still be self-employed but your money will arrive each week with a payslip by cheque or go directly into your bank account.

It is essential to keep track of who owes you money and have the relevant paperwork to go with the job. Don't forget to allow for agent's commission and National Insurance that may get deducted at source, especially if you have spent the money before you receive it! It can be a shock to expect £150 but only get £123.57 because you didn't allow for commission and VAT (any agents that collect payment on your behalf have to charge VAT on commission if they are registered, by law). If you are earning enough income to justify becoming VAT registered, this money can be claimed back as an expense. Your accountant will let you know if or when this is applicable.

Note in your diary the date on which you did a job, the gross amount you are owed and the commission rate you expect to pay.

Then, as you receive it, list down the actual amount you received and the date you got it, keeping a note of the cheque or reference number and when you banked the money. Remember to include overtime payment or travel expenses. For example:

Job description:	Client/ Agent:	Date of job:	Gross fee:	Date payment received:	Deductions:	Balance received:
TOTP	BBC	25/2/00	£400	28/3/00	£70.50	£329.50

It is important to keep on top of your financial situation. If you let it slip because you are preoccupied with dancing, you will end up confused and very probably penniless! Always make notes and write down payment details if no documents are issued. Being misquoted or underpaid can't be rectified without proof.

Self-employed

Being a professional dancer is a thrilling and varied career, but there comes a point when you will have to sit down at a desk and arrange your paperwork. Depending on your circumstances you will be in one of three categories of employment – self-employed, employed by an employer or unemployed. If you are employed and paid on the Pay As You Earn scheme (PAYE) then your tax will have already been deducted by the time you receive your wages (see 'PAYE'). If you are self-employed, however, you will have to pay your own taxes and National Insurance (NI) contributions and submit your accounts to the tax office every year. Accounting for tax is not taught at school or at college and if you manage to understand any of the material sent to you by your tax office when you register, then you'll be doing very well. Ignoring the issue won't do either; one day they will catch up with you and ask you to explain your income. High interest charges will be incurred if you forget about it . . . it won't go away!

Accountants

Unless you have time to fit in a degree course in accountancy you will undoubtedly have to use an accountant to complete the tax forms for you. Paying a professional such as an accountant may seem daunting to you at first and an unnecessary expense –

accountants are notoriously expensive, working on an hourly rate – but a good one will save you money in the long term. They know all the financial loopholes and will be able to tell you the most tax-efficient way to run your affairs, what is tax deductible and what isn't, for example. Having an accountant you trust and can communicate with is essential. Ask around and find one by recommendation only. It is worth choosing one who is familiar with theatre work. Once you have chosen an accountant get a clear idea what it is he needs from you in order to complete your accounts and tax forms. He may ask for details of:

- your annual income
- your expenses
- bank statements
- any savings accounts, PEPs, ISAs, bonds or shares
- investments
- mortgage or rent details
- pensions
- hire purchase (HP) payments
- running costs of a car
- credit cards.

All of these things will help him to build a picture of your financial situation and will affect the amount of tax you end up paying. You may have never even heard of some of the things listed above; don't worry, your accountant will advise you along the way. Once your career is off the ground you may consider trying to buy a property or seek some kind of financial security for the future. Again your accountant will know best and explain all you need to know about pensions and mortgages, but don't get too bogged down with financial responsibilities too early on. You may decide you want to take off on a world cruise for a year, not pay a mortgage! You will know when the time is right for you.

To keep your accountant's fees to a minimum, there are a few steps to follow: when you start working as a freelance professional dancer, write a letter or telephone your nearest tax office (you can find them in the local phone book) and tell them you would like to register for self-employment. Give them your full name and address and your accountant's name and address. This way they will send copies of all correspondence to your accountant too. Give a copy of your letter to your accountant and he will communicate with your tax office to sort out which class of National Insurance you need to pay and get you a schedule D number (this alone is worth paying for an accountant to sort out). This will entitle you to claim back expenses and any emergency tax charged on future jobs. Keep a record of your accounts. You can draw up some columns in a notebook or buy a special accounting book, but they can look quite intimidating with more columns than you really need. If you have a computer, set up a file dedicated to your earnings. List the jobs you have done, the month you received payment and the total you were paid, on a spreadsheet then hand it to your accountant to make sense of (see 'Spreadsheet 1'). Present your accountant with all your bank statements, your completed list of income and expenses, and any other information he may ask for and ask him to complete your tax return within the given period. He will still have a fair amount of work to do, especially as tax is now self-assessed, but if you can record everything and keep organised you will make his job much easier and consequently cheaper for you.

Expenses

Dancers can claim back tax on all kinds of expenses, and receipts must be retained and provided as evidence of expenditure. Keep all your receipts safe and place them together in monthly piles or in envelopes, then about twice a year or every month if you can manage it, sit down and list what you bought, the month you bought it and how much it cost in another book or ideally on another spreadsheet. Below are examples of *some* of the expenses performers are allowed to claim for, providing they are exclusively for the purpose of your work:

- make-up
- accountancy fees
- agent's commission
- hairdressing
- costumes
- cleaning of costumes
- travel and subsistence when on tour
- postage for business, fan mail
- business stationery
- Equity subscription

- photographs and reproductions
- advertising (casting books etc)
- telephone
- television and video
- theatre tickets
- CDs, cassettes, sheet music
- professional publications e.g. *TV Times, The Stage, High Kicks.*

Spreadsheet 2 shows some of the expenses you can claim, listing what you spent on each subject for every month of the year. This is straightforward to do and easy to understand. Most importantly, it will save your accountant hours of rummaging through mounds of receipts and keep his costs down.

PAYE

Sometimes you can be paid by an employer on the PAYE scheme. Tax and deductions are calculated for you and the work is out of your hands. All you have to worry about is covering the costs of living. You will receive a payslip which will explain the amount of tax and NI deducted from the gross amount and you will be left with the balance. The joys of being an employee are unfortunately a rare occurrence in dancing work and I have never heard of a dancer retiring on a company pension.

It is not unusual for a dancer to be self-employed for some work and employed on PAYE for other work. This is not a problem as long as you give all your payslips to your accountant so he can prevent you having to pay tax twice. If you have a schedule D number you can claim back any tax deducted on PAYE jobs. However, National Insurance is a different story and you may end up paying more than one class type of NI for each job. Always keep your accountant informed of career changes and provide him with the relevant paperwork and you won't go far wrong. For more welfare advice on taxation, National Insurance, benefits and pensions for dancers, call your regional Equity office (see 'Listings').

Rosie Cheeks	Income – Yearly totals											Year 1999/2000	
	Apr	May	June	July	Aug	Sept	Oct	Nov	Dec	Jan	Feb	Mar	Total
Television	150.00		350.00		75.00		880.00					150.00	1455.00
Pop promo/video		450.00		250.00				185.00	100.00	65.00		150.00	1200.00
PA/gigs	180.00		200.00		585.00	660.00		65.00				300.00	1990.00
Photographic		60.00	75.00	180.00	135.00			95.00					545.00
Promotional work	435.00			305.00		35.00	400.00				55.00	600.00	1830.00
Panto 99									1800.00	1800.00	350.00		3950.00
Bank Int (Net)													0.00
B Soc Int (Net)		3.95	6.00										9.95
Reimbursements													0.00
TOTAL INCOME													10979.95

Spreadsheet 1

Rosie Cheeks		Outgoings – Yearly totals										Year 1999/2000	
	Apr	May	June	July	Aug	Sep	Oct	Nov	Dec	Jan	Feb	March	Total
Costumes	35.00		7.50			350.00							392.50
Make-up		10.95			14.00			19.60			10.95		55.50
Agents commission	70.00	50.00	49.00			105.00	80.00		350.00				704.00
Accountancy fees	400.00												400.00
Hairdressing			45.00						45.00				90.00
Cleaning costumes		12.00				20.00							32.00
Travel	90.00		65.00	13.00		11.00	65.00	70.00			85.00		399.00
Tour subsistence	25.00		13.00		18.00	10.00		24.00				15.00	105.00
Postage/fan mail	10.00		11.95			15.00			35.00			24.00	95.95
Stationery		6.60		2.95			15.00					11.25	35.80
Equity subs	52.00												52.00
Photographs					90.00						45.00		135.00
Reproduction			88.00										88.00
Casting books							100.00						100.00
Telephone	150.00				150.00				150.00				450.00
Theatre tickets								16.00			32.00		48.00
CDs, cassettes				15.00									15.00
Sheet music		3.95											3.95
The Stage	4.00	4.00	4.00	4.00	4.00	4.00	4.00	4.00	4.00	4.00	4.00	4.00	48.00
TOTAL EXPENSES													3249.70

Spreadsheet 2

Points to remember

- Accept rejection as part of your job.
- Keep hold of your will to succeed and desire to dance during the low times.
- Make use of precious time off when you're not working.
- Get all the details of the job you're doing – refer to your check list.
- Plan ahead for new jobs and pack the items you think you may need.
- Allow extra time for travelling on the first day in case of hold-ups.
- Keep a note of your start and finish time.
- Stay focused on your work and don't judge the situation too early on.
- Keep a record of your income and expense, and file away your receipts.
- Allow for delayed payments and remember commission, VAT and NI.
- Manage your money (make it last) and keep track of who owes you what.
- Don't undercharge – give yourself time to think before you quote fees.
- Get written confirmation for *every* job.
- Get a trustworthy accountant you can communicate with.
- Don't ever ignore your tax returns – everyone has to deal with them at some point.

Chapter Eighteen

Looking after Yourself

Accidents and injuries

It is important to remember that your body is your work and if it doesn't function properly you will end up tired and strained, which may result in injuries. You must endeavour to keep fit and healthy and keep your body supple and maintained. Not only must you be aware of what you do to your body, but where you do it. Always pay attention to the conditions you are dancing under. Is the floor sprung? Is it safe? Can you see where you are going? What happens if you trip on a broken floorboard backstage – is the company employing you covered for insurance? There will inevitably be times in your career when you need the work and the pay, so you jeopardise your precious limbs and take to performing on concrete, but think before you snatch up the work. If an accident occurs it may prevent you from dancing or earning again for a long time, completely defeating the object, and you will never forgive yourself for making such an easy mistake. So try and make sensible decisions about the conditions you are prepared to dance in.

One option is to investigate some personal insurance cover to protect you and your income should anything happen. To find suitable insurance cover for being a dancer will take some research and greatly depend on your circumstances. Equity can recommend relevant insurance brokers and will provide you with the necessary advice for seeking public liability cover, backstage cover or accident insurance. If you are already an Equity member you are covered for all of these on Equity contracts, while many large companies and long contracts also cover their dancers as part of the company insurance, so check this at the time of engagement.

Dealing with injuries

If you are unfortunate enough to injure yourself through landing badly or tired joints for example, regardless of any insurance cover you may have, don't ignore it and hope it will just disappear. Go and get treated as soon as possible and stop dancing immediately until you find out what damage has been done. If you continue to dance on a minor niggle, it will gradually get worse. No matter how small, get it seen to and corrected before it stops you working. Two weeks off work healing a groin strain is far better than a career cut short because of back problems extending from ignoring your disarranged hips. Make sure you seek medical advice. Don't leave it to guess work and throw a bag of frozen peas and a hot water bottle on your twisted ankle and hope for the best. Unless you have a first-aid background, leave it to the experts. You may know a physiotherapist from your training days or your choreographer will provide basic advice, but be sure to see a GP as soon as you can after the event. If your injury happens just as you are about to perform a run through, tell your choreographer you are unable to dance; they will understand. It is not worth ruining your body and your future for, and they will want you fully fit for the performance night. If your injury occurs during a perform-ance, unless it is crucial you probably won't feel the pain or know what you've done until the show's over. Adrenalin and intense concentration will carry you through the performance and you may not realise the full extent of your injury until much later.

You may go through your entire dancing days without an injury, but it is important to know what to do in such circumstances.

Dance UK is an organisation based in London which acts as a voice for the professional dance community (see 'Listings'). It offers a medical register helpline to find a practitioner experi-enced in treating dancers, as well as free advice and information on other areas in the dancing industry, with information sheets on:

Dancer's first-aid box – basic advice for treating *minor* injuries and illnesses.
Care of the instrument – the body as the instrument of a dancer.
Myths and facts about dance and the body – information worth remembering in case of injury.

How to have healthy bones – how to avoid osteoporosis.
Food and nutrition for male and female dancers – how to be healthy and strong.
Muscular imbalance – a common cause of lower back pain in dancers.
Fluids for dancers – the importance of drinking enough.

Health and diet

Staying healthy does not mean staying skinny. It is common for dancers to become rather paranoid about their size and weight, a result of all the time spent watching themselves in front of a full-length mirror and the emphasis placed on image within the business. It is great to make the best of yourself as we've discussed, but if you do suffer from paranoia and always think you look 'fat', then it's time to recondition your mind. Some colleges have been known to put pressure on dancers to adjust their weight, but it's all about eating the right foods at the right time and using the right muscles when you dance. Nobody can get to know your body better than you!

You will hear dancers talk about their metabolic rate and their lack of appetite, but if you have just returned from a weekend at home after three meals a day and a roast dinner to finish, you will be the dancer who can make it through the day without a dizzy spell. Young dancers' bodies take time to settle down, they change as you get older and you will lose or gain weight at different times as you become a young adult. Full-time intense dance training inevitably builds heavy muscle, and muscle weighs more than body fat, so weighing yourself is a definite no-no. It takes a while to learn how to use the correct muscles to lengthen your limbs rather than bunch them up to look like a shot-putter. Eventually you will get to know your body and you can decide what is best for you to eat. We all know the people who have near-to-perfect figures and live on chocolate bars, but are they the fittest? There are also dancers who get through a rehearsal on coffee and cigarettes (they are definitely not the fittest) and then there's the sensible dancer who eats little and often during a physical day and has a diet fortified with vitamins and carbohydrates for energy.

It's so easy for a busy dancer to binge and grab snacks and caffeine boosts for fast energy and easy food. Everyone does it and

Stay healthy!

that's fine on the odd occasion, but long-term effects may be disastrous. The extreme is for dancers to starve themselves, particularly two days prior to a performance, despite the fact that they are half asleep in rehearsals and hospitalised after the performance. To starve yourself drains your body of fluid and essential nutrients that make your body function. If you don't eat anything, your metabolism will just slow down because it has nothing to burn up. You will lose a suitable amount of body fluid before a performance naturally from the effects of adrenalin and nerves. This will help your costume waistline and make you feel good, but it is essential to have eaten a meal a few hours beforehand.

These days there are so many diet books available, all with conflicting information. I remember a few years ago when everybody started food combining, and experts are still trying to prove its results. The answer is to know yourself and know what you need to maintain a healthy lifestyle for dancing and looking good. Understand your body and what it can get away with. If you have a passion for fattening foods, limit them when you are working and treat yourself when you have time off. My answer was to turn vegetarian. All through college I was a bulky dancer, then at 20 I stopped eating meat and slimmed right down. It is a matter of being aware of the right foods to eat and eating in moderation. You should have a general knowledge of vitamins, minerals, proteins and carbohydrates or you can obtain leaflets from your doctor at the time of your medical. Don't swamp yourself with diet books or follow any silly fads you hear about. Your diet will reflect in your skin and your personality; a hungry dancer is a grouchy one, while a healthy dancer is slim and toned with colour in her cheeks. The strongest dancers are not the skinniest, who can look weak, but the ones who perform with power and definition to their lines. Whether you are big or small, good toned bodies and positive movements make attractive dancers to watch.

Apply the following guidelines to your diet:

- eat plenty of carbohydrates for energy – pasta, potatoes, rice, bread
- eat fresh fruit every day for vitamins A, C, and D
- eat steamed, microwaved or raw vegetables for the maximum vitamin intake
- eat dairy or soya (vegan) products for strong teeth and bones
- beware of hidden fats in pastries, cakes, biscuits
- beware of high levels of sugar in sauces, crisps, sweets
- take a vitamin supplement if you are prone to lack of energy or colds
- drink plenty of water every day
- avoid lots of caffeine or cigarettes as they destroy vitamins
- eat fast food and snack bars in moderation
- learn how your own body functions
- eat sensibly and know your body
- don't starve or binge
- be happy with the way you look!

Chapter Nineteen

Hanging up your Shoes!

Retirement

Unfortunately there comes a time when you can't dance as well as you used to, or you don't look young enough to maintain a dancing career. These are normally the signs to call it a day. Unfortunately it is a short-lived career, but there is no set age at which you must retire from dancing. You should just know the signs and continue with your career until they stare you in the face. If you stop too early you will miss it for the rest of your life, unless of course something else comes along that diverts your interest. I remember the day I actually said 'OK, enough is enough!' I was called up for an audition for a new TV comedy show that wanted dancers in their mid-twenties (I was 27), not too skinny, big personalities and prepared to act in sketches – perfect, it was me! Off I went (after a 12-month break from dancing to give birth to my 10lb baby boy), and while I was a little rusty, it felt great to be dancing. The audition progressed and I remember thinking 'This one is in the bag'. The clients and choreographer seemed to be paying me a lot of attention and kept smiling at me. As it got to the final line-up of dancers my name wasn't called and I was asked to leave. It wasn't until I collected my CV and photograph on the way out that I glanced down to see one word written in pencil beside my name: plump. They thought I was plump! Surely my leotard wasn't that tight? But that was when I decided to call it a day.

Some dancers lose their confidence through dragging themselves to uninspiring auditions and dancing next to the latest batch of 18-year-old college graduates. You were there once, and although you felt a nervous wreck you were also ready to tackle the world – green, but incredibly keen! Ten years of experience can allow you to walk auditions and win jobs hands down; clients love to employ experienced, relaxed and reliable dancers as a nervy beginner can cause too much hassle. But if you no longer feel good about yourself or your looks, or if rejection has finally eaten away at you, then give the opportunities to the new faces and take a back seat. Giving up dancing early does not mean you've failed. If you had a career as a dancer then it has all been worth it, but now it's time to explore the possibilities of other work using your knowledge and experience of professional dancing.

A lot of female dancers stop dancing after giving birth because of the physical changes involved. You never quite regain the same dancing body or positive mind after giving birth, although in some cases pregnancy has made dancers more flexible and more centred, making them feel complete as an individual and ready to dance better than before. Remember, there's no set age at which you're suddenly too old to dance. You are judged by your dancing ability and your look in auditions; nobody cares about your age. *You're as old as you feel!*

Moving on

Other areas of the dancing industry may suit the older dancer. When I was pregnant I discovered historical dancing, and although I looked like Humpty Dumpty in a leotard, nobody even suspected my bump under an 18th-century Empire line costume. I was perfect for a Jane Austen ballroom scene and the dancing was so elegant it was a perfect diversion to my commercial dance career. Dancing in period films is suited to all ages as the production must portray the correct era and the people of that time and that includes all ages, shapes and sizes!

Throughout a dancer's career she will work for a number of different companies and get to know how they operate and produce shows from behind the scenes. The team of people who work for such organisations cover a range of talents and qualifications and the dancers in the show are just one element. Numerous dancers are employed for each production and they come and go so fast, but dancers who stay and build a relationship with the companies and mature into business-minded individuals, have the perfect opening to find a new career. It may mean a total change of direction or require a quick computer literacy course, but after years of working for the same people you gain their trust and they get used to you being around. A typical example of this is working for a cruiseliner company – you dance in shows on ships for the same company for a few years, then get promoted to head girl and go on to become assistant choreographer and then choreographer for one ship, then two ships and so on. The recording industry is another favourite. They like to employ trendy, confident people with a creative mind, and any dancer who has worked for pop acts, on band tours, in PAs and videos, will have a basic knowledge of the mechanics of their industry. Teaching dance in state schools or independent dance schools or starting up your own dance studio are also popular choices for retired dancers. The possibilities are endless.

It's easy for a dancer considering retirement to panic about the future, but generally dancers are confident, creative and good communicators and there are so many jobs linked with companies who use dancers. It's quite normal for a dancer to have a blank mind when considering the future because she has spent her life doing what she loves and thinking about change is daunting. There is a whole realm of jobs that require dancing knowledge as part of the skill, including:

- dance teacher (in colleges, studios, stage schools)
- dance therapy (helping individuals cope using movement)
- dance administrators/secretary (for dance organisations or companies)
- dance critic (writing about and commenting on dance productions)
- costume designer
- venue organiser
- co-producing (TV or theatre productions about dance)
- writer (columnist, author)
- dance agent or booker
- physiotherapist for dancers (will involve training)
- masseur for dancers (short courses available to become qualified).

I asked some already retired dancers what they did after hanging up their dancing shoes:

I work for a mobile phone company. It's promotional work, demonstrating the different models of phone and travelling around to exhibitions to set up stands and launch promotions. I miss dancing terribly but it's fab being on a regular wage!

I have been trying to give up for years, but I still pop back to do the odd job when I'm asked. I now work in continuity for a TV production company. They love me and let me have time off for dancing work if we're not in mid-production.

I went on to become an agent and start my own business recruiting dancers. It was a huge challenge, but I had so many contacts from working as a dancer it seemed the obvious choice.

I haven't given up yet, I was about to in the summer and suddenly work picked up and I haven't stopped for weeks. I have been doing a computer course because I intend on going into band management or some kind of marketing in a record company. Most of my dancing work has been for them, so I know a lot about the industry already.

I took all my dancing teaching exams and did an Aerobics Instructor's course, and now that I'm qualified I give lessons in a health club and teach dancing at a local school. I still do extra work and promotional work sometimes to boost my income.

I have established myself as a choreographer. It was difficult at first because I still danced on some jobs, but now I'm older and no longer dance I am taken seriously and have some excellent clients and I do all their shows. I want to be a choreographer forever, I could never move on from the dancing world!

I am now qualified as a script supervisor and currently head of production for a production and facilities company. I didn't appreciate how much I learnt as a dancer – if only I had known, maybe my confidence levels would have been higher!

I have had four children! I don't think I could possibly squeeze in another career, not until they all go to school. I choreograph local productions and teach part-time to keep me dancing, but I'm now a full-time mother.

Listings

Training Colleges

The Arts Educational School
Dance course (two years)
Tring Park
Tring
Hertfordshire HP23 5LX
Tel: 01442 824 255
Fax: 01442 891 069

The Arts Educational School
Musical Theatre and Dance course
(three years)
Cone Ripman House
14 Bath Road
London W4 1LY
Tel: 020 8987 6666

Central School of Ballet
Professional Performers' course
(three years)
Classical Ballet and related subjects
(three years)
10 Herbal Hill
Clerkenwell Road
London EC1R 5EJ
Tel: 020 7837 6332
Fax: 020 7833 5571

Doreen Bird
Dance and Theatre Performance
Diploma (three years)
Birbeck Centre
Birbeck Road
Sidcup
Kent DA14 4DE
Tel: 020 8300 6004

Elmhurst School for Dance and Performing Arts
Vocational training
Heathcote Road
Camberley
Surrey GU15 2EW
elmhurst@cableol.co.uk
Tel: 01276 65301
Fax: 01276 670320

Elmhurst offers two courses, each of three years' duration for students aged 16–19. The Classical Ballet and Performing Arts course and the Dance and Performing Arts programme provide professional training for those seeking employment in the classical, contemporary and commercial dance sector. Graduates are highly successful in securing professional work on the completion of their training and ex-Elmhurst students are to be found working in major ballet companies in this country and abroad as well as in West End musical theatre productions. Further details and application forms may be obtained from the Admissions Secretary at the school.

English National Ballet School
Intensive Classical Ballet course
(two years)
Carlyle Building
Hortensia Road
London SW10 OQS
Tel: 020 7376 7076
Fax: 020 7376 3404

The Hammond School
The Hammond Diploma in Dance
Performance and Teaching
(three years)
Mannings Lane
Chester CH2 2PB
Tel: 01244 400 143
Fax: 01244 315 845

√ The Italia Conti Academy of Theatre Arts Ltd
Performing Arts diploma course (three years)
23 Goswell Road
London EC1M 7AJ
Tel: 020 7608 0047
Fax: 020 7253 1430

Laban Centre for Movement and Dance
BA (Hons) Dance Theatre
(three years)
Laurie Grove Diploma in Dance
Theatre (three years)
New Cross
London SE14 6NJ
Tel: 020 8692 4070

Laine Theatre Arts Ltd
Musical Theatre, Performers' and
Teachers' course (three years)
The Studios
East Street
Epsom
Surrey KT17 1HH
Tel: 01372 724 648

London Contemporary Dance School
BA (Hons) Contemporary Dance
(three years)
The Place
16 Flaxman Terrace
London WC1H 9AB
Tel: 020 7387 0152

London Studio Centre
Theatre Dance course (Dip or BA
(Hons)) (three years)
42–50 York Way
London N1 9AB
Tel: 020 7837 7741
Fax: 020 7837 3248

Merseyside Dance and Drama Centre
The Teacher and Performance course
for Dance and Musical Theatre
(three years)
The Studios
13–17 Camden Street
Liverpool L3 8JR
Tel: 0151 207 6197

Midlands Academy of Dance and Drama
Musical Theatre course (three years)
50 Cornhill Road
Carlton
Nottingham NG4 1GE
Tel/Fax: 0115 911 0401

Northern Ballet School
Professional Dancers' course
(three years)
Dance Teachers' Diploma course
(three years)
The Dancehouse
10 Oxford Road
Manchester M1 5QA
Tel: 0161 237 1406
Fax: 0161 237 1408

Performers' College
The Performers' Theatre Dance course
(three years)
2–4 Chase Road
Corringham
Essex SS17 7QH
Tel: 01375 672 053
Fax: 01375 672 353

Rambert School
The Professional Diploma course
(three years)
Brunel University College
Twickenham Campus
300 St Margaret's Road
Twickenham
Middlesex TW1 1PT
Tel: 020 8891 0121

College of the Royal Academy
of Dancing
The Art and Teaching of Ballet BA
(Hons) (three years)
36 Battersea Square
London SW11 3RA
Tel: 0171 223 0091

Stella Mann College
Dance course for Performers/Teachers
(three years)
343a Finchley Road
Hampstead
London NW3 6ET
Tel: 020 7435 9317
Fax: 020 7435 3782

Studio La Pointe
Teacher Training and Performing
Arts Diploma course (three years)
5 Chapel Lane
Garforth
Leeds LS25 1AG
Tel: 0113 286 8136
Fax: 0113 287 4487

The Urdang Academy
Performers' Diploma course
(three years)
20–22 Shelton Street
Covent Garden
London WC2H 9JJ
Tel: 0171 836 5709
Fax: 0171 836 7010

Professional dance classes and rehearsal studios

Custard Factory
Gibb Street
Digbeth
Birmingham B9 4AA
Tel: 0121 604 7777

Dance Attic Studios
Fulham Old Baths
368 North End Road
London SW6 1LY
Tel: 020 7610 2055

Danceworks
16 Balderton Street
London W1
Tel: 020 7629 6183

Global Vibrations
38 Glenloch Road
London NW3 4DN
Tel: 020 7419 007

Holborn Centre
Three Cups Yard Off Sandland Street
London WC1
Tel: 020 7405 5334

Islington Arts Factory
2 Parkhurst Road
London N7
Tel: 020 7607 056

Pineapple Dance Studio
7 Langley Street
London WC2
Tel: 020 7836 4004

Agents

Dancing work

Acrobats Unlimited
The Circus Space
Coronet Street
London N1 6HD
Tel: 020 7613 5259

Dancers
1 Charlotte St
London W1P 1DH
Tel: 020 7636 1473
Fax: 020 7636 1657

The Eastman Marley Organisation (EMO)
7th Floor
54–62 Regent Street
London W1R 5PJ
Tel: 020 7439 4052
Fax: 020 7287 2844

The Essential Agency Ltd
(non-exclusively represents dancers/singers/choreographers/actors)
368 North End Road
London SW6 1LY
essltd@aol.com
Tel: 020 7385 2460
Fax: 020 7610 0995

Recruitment auditions advertised in The Stage. Postal details accepted – send photo, CV and covering letter with SAE. Applicants will be invited for audition/interview or kept on file. Showreels (with SAE) welcome.

Michael Summerton Management
336 Fulham Road
London SW10 9UG
Tel: 020 7351 7777
Fax: 020 7352 0411

Pineapple Agency
44 Earlham Street
London WC2H 9LA
Tel: 020 7241 6601
Fax: 020 7379 4072

Scot-Baker Agency
(representsdancers/models/ choreographers)
35 Caithness Road
Brook Green
London W14 0JA
scot.baker@btinternet.com
Tel: 020 7603 9988
Fax: 020 7603 7698

All applicants in the first instance must write to the agency enclosing a photograph, CV and SAE (large enough to return the photo if necessary) for a reply. The agency usually holds auditions to join the books once/twice a year.

Success
Suite 74, 3rd Floor, Kent House
87 Regent Street
London W1R 7HF
Tel: 020 7734 3356
Fax: 020 7494 3787

Tommy Tucker Agency
43 Drury Lane
London WC2B 5RT
Tel: 020 7497 2113
Fax: 020 7379 0451

Trends
54 Lisson Street
London NW1 6ST
Tel: 020 7723 8001
Fax: 020 7258 3591

Television commercial, photographic and acting work

Broad Casting Co
Unit 23 Canalot Studios
222 Kensal Road
London W10 5BN
Tel: 020 7460 5222

Crawfords
2 Conduit Street
London W1R 9TG
Tel: 020 7629 6464

Galloways One
15 Lexham Mews
London W8 6JW
Tel: 020 7376 2288

Lookalikes
26 College Crescent
London NW3 5LH
Tel: 020 7387 9245

Mugshots
20 Greek Street
London
W1V 5LF
Tel 020 7437 2275

Modelling

Bodyline Model Agency
32 Akeman Street
Tring
Herts HP23 6AN
Tel: 01442 890490

Models One
Omega House
471 Kings Road
London SW10 0LU
Tel: 020 7351 1195

MOT Model Agency
The Stables
Ashlyns Hall
Chesham Road
Berkhamstead Herts HP4 2ST
Tel: 01442 863918
Fax: 01442 873333

Nevs
Regal House
198 Kings Road
London SW3 5XX
Tel 020 7352 7273

Select
43 Kings Street
London WC2E 8RJ
Tel: 020 7470 5200

Storm
5 Jubilee Place
London SW3 3TD
Tel: 020 7352 2278

Top Models
3rd Floor
21 Goldhawk Road
London W12 8QQ
Tel: 020 8743 0640

Uglies/Rage Models
Tigris House
256 Edgware Road
London W2 1DS
Tel: 020 7402 5564

Extra work

The David Agency
153 Battersea Rise
London SW11 1HP
Tel: 020 7223 7720

Dolly Brook Casting Agency
52 Sandford Road
East Ham
London E6 3QS
Tel: 020 8472 2561

G2
15 Lexham Mews
London W8 6JW
Tel: 020 7376 2133

JB Agency
7 Stonehill Mansions
8 Streatham High Road
London SW16 1DD
Tel: 020 8677 5151

Lee's People
238 Nelson Road
Middlesex TW2 7BW
lee@lees-people.co.uk
Tel: 020 8898 9000

Ray Knight Casting
21A Lambolle Place
Belsize Park
London NW3 4PG
Tel: 020 7722 4111

Promotional work

Aesthetics
43 Trossachs Road
Mount Nod
Coventry CV5 YBJ
Tel: 01203 462620

Anna Savva Promotions
Glan Llyn
North Street
Caerwys, Flintshire
North Wales CH7 AW
Tel: 01352 720 080

Mainline International
Kingsdown House
Green Lane
Corley Moor
Coventry CV7 8AL
Tel: 01676 540 451

PPM Promotions
The Cottage
Main Street,
Sutton-on-the-forest
York Y061 1DW
Tel: 07000 776776

Cabaret work

AMG
11–13 Broadcourt
Covent Garden
London WC2B 5QN
Tel: 020 7240 5652

BCM
Agency House
6 Park Drive
Derby DE7 5NR
Tel: 0115 932 8615

Wally Dent Entertainments
121a Woodlands Avenue
West Byfleet
Weybridge
Surrey KT14 6AS
Tel: 01932 347 885

Photographers

Experienced in taking dancers'
publicity shots.

Brandon Bishop
28/29 Great Sutton Street
London EC1V 0DS
Tel: 020 7253 5868/0374 289 522

Sergio Bondioni
Yellow Brick Studio
4B Lonsdale Road
London NW6 6RD
Tel: 020 7624 4589

Jon Clarke
Unit C51
17–19 Westferry Road
London E14 8JH
Tel: 020 7538 3804

Printers

For Z cards and reproductions.

Jon Clarke
Unit C51
17–19 Westferry Road
London E14 8JH
Tel: 020 7538 3804

Denbry Repros
27 John Adam Street
London WC2N 6HX
Tel: 020 7930 1372/020 7839 6496

Denman Repros
33 Upper Parliament Street
Nottingham NG1 2BP
Tel: 0115 947 3257

Eyecatchers
The Studios
Parham Road
Canterbury
Kent CT1 1DE
Tel: 01227 459007/8

Visualeyes
24 West Street
London WC2H 9NA
imaging@visualeyes.ltd.uk
Tel: 020 7836 3004

Associations and organisations

Association of Model Agents
122 Brompton Road
London SW3 1JE
Info. line: 0891 517 644

**Association of Professional
Theatre for Young People**
Unicorn Arts Centre
Great Newport Street
London WC2H 7JB
Tel: 020 7836 3623

**British Actors' Equity
Association**
(trade union representing performers)
Guild House
Upper St Martin's Lane
London WC2H 9EG
info@equity.org.uk
Tel: 020 7379 6000
Fax: 020 7379 7001

**British Association of
Choreographers**
98 Elmhurst Crescent
London N2 OLP
Tel/Fax: 020 8883 8723

The British Council
11 Portland Place
London W1N 4EJ
Tel: 020 7389 3010

**Council for Dance Education
and Training (CDET)**
Studio Eight
The Glasshouse
49A Goldhawk Road
London W12 8QP
cdet@btconnect.com
Tel: 020 8746 0076
Fax: 020 8746 1937

Dance UK
23 Crisp Road
London W6 9RL
Tel: 020 8741 1932

Equity regional offices:

Glasgow	Tel: 0141 248 2472
Manchester	Tel: 0161 832 3183
Cardiff	Tel: 01222 397 971
Warwick	Tel: 01926 408 638
Sheffield	Tel: 01142 305 294

**International Dance Teachers
Association**
76 Bennett Road
Brighton BN2 5JL
info@idta.co.uk
Tel: 01273 685652
Fax: 01273 674388

*The public can apply to the IDTA for
a list of schools in their area without
charge. Further information i
available on training to be a
dancer/dance teacher. Full training
programmes are available through
qualified dance teachers and experienced
choreographers. Literature is available
for those wishing to qualify as dance
teachers with the association. There is a
full back-up information service on
subjects relating to teaching dance.*

Glossary

Dancers are notorious for using jargon and 'in words'. Many of these are listed below along with some technical terms you may not yet know.

AD Abbreviation of Assistant Director. ADs are not normally hidden in the control room on film sets, and often they give out instructions on behalf of the director.

Background artiste Extra work or a supporting artiste – there are many versions and for correct definitions of each consult Equity. Basically all background artistes are used to make a filming situation look real (sitting on a bus, in a hairdresser, at a desk) and pad out the shot.

Bill The order of performances or acts to be seen. There is usually a top of the bill, which is the star turn for the evening. If a billing order is written on a poster you can tell the size of the act by the size of the print: the bigger the act, the bigger the print.

Black-listed A title given to companies and artistes when they have done wrong. Their name is condemned and warnings are given before you get involved with them (for example clients who haven't paid artistes for work already done).

Blag Slang for talking yourself into something or getting round someone by being cheeky and exaggerating a situation to sound better than it is.

Booth singers Back-up vocalists who sing from a booth off-stage to enhance the sound on stage.

Buy out The alternative to repeat fees – a one-off payment given to an artiste who features in a shot that will be shown repeatedly.

Call time The time you are given to arrive at a job – it may be hours before you do anything, but you must be on site by your given call time for their piece of mind (especially for live performances).

Check in A phone call to remind someone you are available, find out some information or just touch base.

Consummation To communicate with the customers intimately. It is a form of hostess work. You are encouraged to make conversation with the customers and flirt with them.

Continuity In film and TV it is the uninterrupted succession of things, for example if an actress has a red jumper on for scene one she can't then be seen in a green jumper in the same scene. It must be continuous.

Control room A room that resembles an aeroplane cockpit tucked away in a TV or recording studio. It's full of highly technical equipment and is where they 'make things happen'!

Date sheet Like a calendar, but adapted to show dates/gigs at a glance. It is used a lot for touring so you know where you are on what day.

Dep A person who acts as substitute for another. Similar to a stand-in or understudy.

Digs list A list of accommodation available near a venue, giving a variety of types (hotel/B&B/guest house etc.) and prices.

Gigs An engagement or single performance you are paid to do (unlike PAs which are often freebies).

Hang up Dancers' jargon for an insecurity. If you're hung up about something, you're worried about it or think you're no good at it.

Hooking up Slang for meeting with someone or joining together for a particular venture.

Kicked out A phrase used by dancers when they have been asked to leave an audition at a certain point. You may get down to the last two and still get 'kicked out'.

Luvvies A nickname given to the-atricals – people who are swept up in the drama of the industry!

On spec Slang for a speculation without being certain of the out-come.

Pas de deux Stemming from clas-sical ballets where the ballerina dances with her cavalier, it generally means a female and male dancing together. These days dancers use the term 'partner work'.

Per diem Latin for per day. An amount of money paid each day to an artiste to cover living expenses if they are not already provided and the artiste is away from home (meals, travel etc.).

Playing range The ages you think you can look. If you are 23 you may be able to look 18–28 (actors sometimes include this on their CV).

Press release A sheet or package of information about an act or production that is circulated around the industry and media.

Run A name given to the total length of the period a production is on for.

Run through A rehearsal of the complete performance from start to finish, preferably without stopping.

Shoots The name given to photography sessions (filmed or still).

Stage school A school specifically designed for children aged 5–16 to learn to be on the stage and where performing skills are considered equally as important as academic. The timetable will reflect both areas and national curriculum exams are taken.

Stills Photographic shots that are not filmed but individual frames.

Take When the clapperboard sounds and someone yells 'take one!' It is an instance of photogra-phy – they are filming a section and the camera is rolling until the direc-tor says, 'Cut!'.

Usage The approval given for a photograph to be used around the world or sold on without causing problems.

Index